IN LIVING COLOR:

AN ANTHOLOGY OF CONTEMPORARY STUDENT WRITINGS ON RACE

Edited By: Karen Reardon, Megan Schoen and Jaime Longo

Written By: Past and Present Students of La Salle University with Invited Contributions from Faculty

Copyright © 2020 Karen Reardon, Megan Schoen and Jaime Longo

Individual writing and images included by permission of each author.

Cover image: *Might Could* (2000) by Moe Brooker (b. 1940). Oil and pastel on paper, 30" by 30". Purchased with funds provided by Michael Duffy, Dr. Helen North, Dr. Dennis O'Brien, and the Morrow-Farrell Family (in memory of Theodore Eggleston Morrow), Collection of La Salle University Art Museum, 05-D-414. Artwork © Moe Brooker.

All rights reserved by their respective copyright holders. For permission to reproduce any of the material in this volume, please contact Karen Reardon at: reardonk@lasalle.edu or findagreement@aol.com

ISBN: 9781711807829

IN LIVING COLOR:

AN ANTHOLOGY OF CONTEMPORARY STUDENT WRITINGS ON RACE

TABLE OF CONTENTS

Preface · 1
Acknowledgments · 2
Foreword · 4
A Note on Editing · 7

Faculty Frames

Luisa Ossa, PhD — *Reflections on Race* · 9

Brian Henderson, FSC — *Reflection on the Important Power of an Anthology on Race* · 13

Rosemary Barbera, PhD, MSS. — *Bearing Witness to White Supremacy from Inside* · 16

Charles Gallagher, PhD — *Navigating Racial Schizophrenia in an Era of Colorblindness* · 20

Karen Reardon, PhD, JD — *Diversity Management: Legal and Ethical Challenges for Aspiring Workplace Leaders* · 26

Sara Shuman, PhD, MPH — *Racism and Health Disparities: The Role of Health Care Professionals* · 28

Ernest Miller, FSC, DMin — *On Mission: Let Us Not Grow Weary in Doing What is Right* · 31

Student Writing Units

Unit 1: Wake Up! We Have A Problem	35
Unit 2: Race And America: Is It Learned? Could It Be About Fear and Power?	69
Unit 3: Being "Black"	85
Unit 4: Prejudice and Discrimination: Beyond Black and White	105
Unit 5: Overcoming Bias: Confronting and Confirming	127
Unit 6: The Professional as Witness: Journalism	143
Unit 7: Hope: Finding the Inspiration, the Tools to Fight On	169
Teaching Notes and Appendices	203
About the Cover Art, Artist	210
Postscript	212

DEDICATION

To the legacy of Dr. Martin Luther King, Jr. and those who understand—or we hope will come to understand that

Our lives begin to end
the day we become silent about things that matter.

—*Dr. Martin Luther King, Jr.*

PREFACE

In Living Color: An Anthology of Contemporary Student Writings on Race is a compilation of recent college student perspectives from La Salle University on the contentious and deeply divisive issue of race in the United States of America. Collected between 2014-2017, the works offer a broad range of reflections on race, privilege, prejudice, and systemic racism witnessed and experienced by university students today.

Through writings composed both inside and outside their coursework, students share their voices in multiple genres—including research articles, poetry, personal essays, artwork, and multimedia projects. Faculty and staff introductions provide scholarly frameworks for the students' experiences and represent many disciplines across the university. At the heart of this book is a commitment to the principles of student-centered learning and social justice that pervade education in the Lasallian tradition.

This anthology contains works appropriate to assign in college-level classes across the curriculum, in both undergraduate and graduate programs, as well as in high schools. Whether you teach within arts and sciences, business, nursing and health sciences, or other fields, In Living Color contains readings relevant to your classes. While created in the context of a Lasallian school, this text could be used productively by any university or high school educators interested in amplifying students' voices about race. Readings in this book can be assigned for faculty development activities, student organizations, campus and community events, and themed initiatives including student retreats and orientations. Likewise, this Anthology is suitable for use in corporate and professional workshops and retreats focused on diversity and inclusion and to encourage empathy.

This important and timely collection invites us all as citizens of the world to enter into conversation with the student, faculty and staff authors, continuing the challenging, but necessary work performed within these pages.

ACKNOWLEDGEMENTS

The editors wish to acknowledge the many people whose inspirations and contributions made this Anthology possible. We first recognize the La Salle University Ferguson and Beyond faculty/staff group. The group met during the 2014-2015 academic year to plan campus responses to the mounting stories of police brutality against people of color throughout the country. It was from those discussions that this Anthology was born. When Karen proposed an idea at a Ferguson and Beyond meeting to compile students' writings about race, Marjorie Allen, then Director of Integrative Studies, suggested that Karen team up with Jaime and Megan. We therefore owe Marjie a debt of gratitude for forging this productive partnership. Thank you also to Maggie McGuinness, former Vice President of Mission, who listened attentively and gave us sage advice and encouragement about the Anthology's potential directions at the earliest stages of the project's development.

We deeply appreciate Heather McGee, then Director of Service Learning and the Greater Philadelphia Initiative, who provided prize money for contest awards to help incentivize student submissions as we solicited contributions and assembled the Anthology. Heather also served as the reader of our manuscript offering commentary and teaching questions which greatly enhanced our work. Many thanks are due Tara Carr-Lemke, Director of the Explorer Connection, who allowed us to publicize the Anthology at an Explorer Café. Tara and Heather's assistance with supporting and promoting the Anthology was invaluable.

We also want to recognize Huntly Collins for helping craft the introduction to Unit 6 featuring several pieces originally written by La Salle students for Germantown Beat and for providing that student writing to us, resulting in the unit dedicated to student journalism. Similarly, we recognize the contribution of Whitney Howell who identified an important piece of student writing for inclusion in the Anthology and contributed the inspired assignment she crafted which resulted in that work.

We appreciate the assistance of Rebecca Oviedo and the La Salle Art Museum for introducing us to celebrated artist Moe Brooker who so graciously permitted us to use his beautiful work "Might Could" for the Anthology cover. We were inspired by the piece, struck by the complex beauty created from many colors, which has a profoundly joyful quality about it. We thought it a metaphor for the respectful complex conversations—from many vantage points—we envision the student writing showcased in the Anthology will inspire. It is our sincere hope that those conversations will lead readers to appreciate and respect not only our different experiences of race, but also our common humanity.

We thank all our wonderful La Salle University colleagues who supported and encouraged us throughout the long process of publication. We regret that we cannot mention all by name. In particular, several La Salle faculty and staff members contributed critical and personal perspectives to frame or provide creative direction for the Anthology, and we are grateful for their insights and disciplinary expertise. The Anthology includes faculty frames from Luisa Ossa, Rosi Barbera, Brother Brian Henderson, Karen Reardon, Sara Shuman, Charles Gallagher and Brother Ernest Miller as well as a postscript from the writing of Brother Robert Kinzler for the La Salle King's Dream Committee. We benefitted from the creative direction of Joshua Ash during the campaign soliciting student submissions. We appreciate their time and effort in making these contributions that greatly strengthen the book.

We wish to thank the King's Dream Committee, which sponsors the Martin Luther King Speech and Spoken Word Event at La Salle. Those passionate student voices inspired the Anthology. Most of all, we acknowledge the La Salle University students who lifted their voices and shared their experiences of the complicated, messy, and often painful issues surrounding race and racial relations in the United States today which comprise the Anthology. We applaud their courage in entering and continuing this conversation. We value the ongoing discussion we know their writings will inspire among future students at La Salle University and elsewhere, including other Lasallian institutions where social justice—including racial justice—is central to the mission.

FOREWORD

Each year, the La Salle Community honors the legacy of Dr. Martin Luther King, Jr. in a variety of ways, including through a dedicated community service, an ecumenical prayer service and an oratory contest. Over some years, the oratory contest inspired students of diverse racial and ethnic backgrounds to give impassioned presentations about citizenship, race, service, social justice and the meaning Dr. King's work, still unfinished, holds for us today. In attendance at the contest, I found myself a bit sad observing that such important messages were being delivered to such a small audience. I began to think about how one might build a larger audience for student rhetoric.

In the classroom too, I observed that when offered a choice, students in my business law classes often were writing about race in response to the killing of Trayvon Martin and the other events that followed which collectively gave birth to the "Black Lives Matter" movement. The writing by students of many races and ethnicities showed a keen interest in and insights about their own lived experience and that of others around issues such as employment discrimination and affirmative action, as well as encounters with police and the criminal justice system. Their sentiment was important—too important it seemed to be consumed merely by an audience of one instructor in exchange for a grade. With student agreement, I began to collect these writings.

When an ad hoc faculty committee met to consider how, as faculty, we might respond to and teach about incidents such as Ferguson and other contemporary events across disciplines, I shared my concern that there were limited opportunities for student voices on these pressing issues to be heard and my initial attempt to begin collecting student writing. I was touched and encouraged by the enthusiasm my colleagues Megan Schoen and Jaime Longo showed for the idea of an anthology of student writing and inspired by their expressed willingness to work on the project.

Together, we launched the Anthology shortly thereafter. We began by reaching out to students who had spoken in the oratory competitions to contribute their pieces. We followed with outreach to faculty across disciplines whom we asked to nominate student classroom submissions for inclusion. We expanded the search for contributions through a student writing competition sponsored by La Salle's service learning programs. We advertised the competition through the use of a flyer posted on the university portal as well as through direct communication with faculty to seek their assistance in encouraging student submissions. We attended university workshops which dealt with issues of race to share information about the Anthology and writing competition in order to encourage submissions. Ultimately, we awarded prizes for the top submission in four categories: Academic Research, Poetry, Prose, and Mixed Media.

We hosted an "Explorer Café," a university workshop which invited students to read and discuss selections from the forthcoming Anthology. We awarded the writing competition awards there and spoke about the origins of the project. The space for the workshop was staged as an art gallery, modelled after the concept of a poetry gallery conceived by management educators Van Buskirk and London. We displayed student writing on the walls of the room, including selected passages of longer works. Participants were invited to roam the "gallery" much like they would at a museum. We encouraged everyone to read and reflect on the student contributions. After a time, participants were invited to select a writing to read aloud in small groups and to share reactions and perspectives if they felt comfortable doing so. Sharing was voluntary. Participants were given permission simply to listen. The exercise concluded by inviting all participants back to the full group to share thoughts, feelings and take-aways for awareness or action. We thanked everyone for their participation and encouraged students to consider whether they had a writing they might provide to the Anthology project.

In order to frame the issues on race addressed by the student writing, we also invited contributions from faculty that make explicit and communicate the connection to mission as well as to teaching and learning. Thus, the Anthology includes faculty commentary that share academic and personal reflections on race as a construct; the importance that artistic expression has in conveying ideas as well as emotion; the critical importance of the privileged as witness to and herald of injustice to others; and the connection to mission of both the Christian Brothers religious order and our Lasallian university.

We envision this Anthology as a teaching tool for students at La Salle University and beyond. The student work is loosely organized by theme and accompanied by unit questions that could be used as homework assignments or to otherwise prompt class discussion. We designed the questions to prompt students to engage with the material through self-reflection, but also to go beyond their personal responses to put the texts in conversation with other texts encountered in the unit, with other texts encountered in the Anthology more broadly, and potentially with other texts encountered in a course. The faculty contributions ground the Anthology within academic fields and function as disciplinary frames through which courses across the curriculum could engage with these texts. Though we originally intended the Anthology for use in college classrooms, we believe that the material, though certainly provocative, could lead to beneficial conversations in high schools as well. Likewise, this material could be used in facilitating workplace and community workshops and retreats on the value of diversity, inclusion, and empathy. All proceeds from the sale of the Anthology (net of publication costs) are designated for the benefit of mission-based diversity and inclusion initiatives of La Salle University.

I am beyond grateful for my co-editors Megan Schoen and Jaime Longo for the countless hours they contributed to the Anthology's production. Strangers to me when this project began, I am blessed to count them as friends and so admire their intellectual gifts and generous spirits. I appreciate that the La Salle Ferguson and Beyond Committee facilitated our coming together on this important project. We wish to express appreciation to the student authors, faculty and artist Moe Brooker who volunteered their work, without compensation, so that others might learn. All proceeds from the publication are earmarked to support La Salle University's mission-oriented initiatives.

For me, this work is not merely academic, but *very* personal. As the white mother to two black sons, I stand as witness to the racial injustice they experience almost daily. I have watched the emotional and psychological harm done as they were been spat on, called the "n" word, endured job discrimination or described as "frightening" by persons in white communities encountering a black person for the first time. I have seen them beam, as any child should, when complimented for the respect and manners they display or on the occasions when they show generosity and kindness or speak eloquently on stage. Like Dr. King, I want for my sons and their children to live in a world where "they will not be judged by the color of their skin, but by content of their character." While there is still so much work to be done for us to see that world, I refuse to live without hope.

I know I speak for Jaime and Megan in appreciating and thanking you, our readers, for your willingness to reflect on the thoughts expressed in the pages which follow with an open mind and heart—and your courage to refuse to "remain silent about things that matter."

Karen A. Reardon, PhD, JD

A Note on Editing

This anthology emphasizes the importance and value of student voices on race. Our goal as editors of this anthology was not to achieve unity of perspective or uniformity of style. The student submissions offer a wide range of arguments and viewpoints expressed through a variety of written and visual genres. While all of the anthologized works offer important contributions to an ongoing conversation about race, the writers and artists are not all equally grounded in history, theory, and intersectionality. Their perspectives are often deliberately thought-provoking, seeking to push readers out of their comfort zones, and thus are not always in harmony with each other, with the views of the editors, or with the views of La Salle University. All of the pieces offer powerful testimony, and they do so by privileging each author's and artist's unique voice, voices that we do not wish to blunt or to polish beyond recognition. We have therefore opted to edit with a light hand. We corrected obvious typos and made minor grammatical edits only in places where meaning was affected; when possible, we confirmed the intended meaning with the author. We did not alter stylistic choices, including uses of so-called "non-standard" English. We did not revise all submissions to conform to a single style guide, but rather allowed for the diversity of formats found in different academic disciplines to shine through. We did not correct factual errors, though we are aware that they exist. We did not add citations when none were provided in the original, though we preserved all citations and discursive notes present in the original documents. In one instance, we added a footnote to identify a contemporary public event reference in the student submission, augmented an unclear reference in consultation with the student author, and redacted a writing as directed by a student author to preserve anonymity. It is our hope that, as a result of these decisions, *In Living Color: Contemporary Student Writings on Race* preserves the authenticity of our students' voices in all their diversity.

FACULTY FRAMES

Reflections on Race
Luisa Marcela Ossa, PhD
Associate Professor of Spanish

What is race? Is it based on physical characteristics? Is it based on ancestry and heritage? Is it based on shared interest? Or is it merely a social construct, with no factual base?

Many claim that with the election of President Obama, the U.S. has become a "post-racial" society. They believe that the election of our country's first "black" president marks the end of racism in the U.S. and proves that anyone can achieve anything in our country. Yet in a country where young black males are 21 times more likely to be shot to death by police than their white counterparts[1]; in a country where a college fraternity uses racial slurs to proudly chant about excluding black men from membership[2]; when those who wish to discuss these issues are frequently told they are "too sensitive" or that *THEY* are in fact the racists, how "post-racial" are we really? But I digress, for how can I speak of racism if I have not yet defined race...

According to the Merriam-Webster dictionary, race may be defined as, "a family, a tribe, people, or nation belonging to the same stock," but it may also be defined as, "a class or kind of people unified by shared interests, habits or characteristics." A third definition offered is, "a category of humankind that shares certain distinctive traits." So what do we mean when we speak of race? The first definition? The second? The latter? All of the above? Or is it none of the above?

President Obama is generally described as our nation's first "black" President. Is this due to his physical characteristics? Or is it due to his ancestry; his family? His father was a black man from Kenya, but his mother was a white woman from Kansas. So is he still our nation's first "black" President? Does his mother's "race" and background have no bearing on his? Or does he have a complex identity that encompasses a diverse background that is not either/or?

My skin is light, and my hair is long and thin with a slight wave. My father is a fair-skinned Colombian man of predominantly European ancestry, while my mother was a "black" woman from the United States. Our ancestors are from a long line of people of African descent. But my skin is light and my hair is thin and wavy, so am I not black? Is not my mother still my mother?

Can I embrace my African heritage and still be a multi-racial Colombian-American?

Who gets to decide and define how we are categorized racially? Must it always be an either/or proposition? There are those who say that from a biological standpoint, race does not exist, that it is merely a social construct. However, does this argument in any way negate the existence of the social construct? The fact is that the social construct of race exists, and it has been a pervasive part of U.S. society since this country's inception. While the labor of African-Americans, both enslaved and free was used to build the White House and the U.S. Capitol[3], Native Americans were being forcibly removed from their lands and placed on reservations. [4] The legacy of reservations remains, as approximately 22% of Native Americans still live on reservations, and 38% of those people live below the poverty line.[5] And as Native Americans face this societal marginalization, an NFL team continues to call itself the Redskins, despite the fact that many Native Americans find the term offensive. Meanwhile, the mainstream media hosts debates to "decide" whether Native Americans should be offended by the term or not.

So let us return to the definitions of race: "a family, a tribe, people, or nation belonging to the same stock; a class or kind of people unified by shared interests, habits or characteristics;" or "a category of humankind that shares certain distinctive traits." Do any of these definitions imply worth? Intrinsically, no. Yet our society has used race to define human value. While Native Americans were found unworthy of being a part of the formation of this country and of being a part of its mainstream society and, therefore, were placed on reservations, enslaved black people were priced from $0- to approximately $1500 based on factors such as age, gender, and physical attributes, among others.[6] This begs the question, why must a value of better or lesser be placed on human beings based on race? Why can't difference just be difference, without the implication of better or worse?

Over the weeks that I prepared this essay I thought to myself, where do I go with this essay? What am I trying to say? Where do I take all of this information that I have? I don't have all of the answers, what can I add to our society's discussion of race, a topic that has been discussed and debated again and again and again…. As I wrote and pondered, I happened across the article "Even an Earthquake Can't Stir Student Empathy" in *The Chronicle of Higher Education*. In the piece, Professor Ranjan Adiga, who is Nepalese, laments the fact that he received no empathy from his students after the April 25, 2015 earthquake in Nepal. Adiga tells how he was supposed to bring doughnuts to a study session he was facilitating for his students but that he forgot because he was consumed with worry for his family and friends in Nepal after learning of the earthquake. When he arrived at the session and announced that he had forgotten the doughnuts because of the earthquake, most of the students had no idea what he was talking about. When he asked one of the few students who was aware of the earthquake what she thought, she responded with a "lazy shrug" and said, 'Sorry, it's Monday morning.' Meanwhile, in the comments section below the article, while many expressed their concern regarding Professor Adiga's experience, others implied that he was speaking unfairly about all Americans, even though in his essay he focuses on his experiences with students at his particular college. One commenter in particular accuses him of being Anti-American stating, "Why would this Nepalese – a beneficiary of a terrific career opportunity in the US—figuratively spit on his American friends?" So while I **DID** empathize with Adiga, and felt sadness for the fact that during a time so difficult and painful for him and for the country of Nepal as a whole, his students solely expressed ignorance of the earthquake or indifference toward it, I also felt troubled and saddened by the comments and lack of empathy by some of the commenters, such as the above cited. And as all of these thoughts and feelings swirled around in my being, it finally struck me that maybe the answer to many of the issues around race is simply, empathy….

So often when the member of one race or type of racial background such as mixed race shares his or her experiences with discrimination, segregation, isolation, or feeling unwelcome, those of another race or background often respond dismissively, with statements such as, "that's not true." Many others respond defensively, taking a stance of, "I personally haven't done anything to you, so why are you telling me?" Other people choose to go on the attack by accusing those who bring up issues of racial injustice (or insensitivity to global issues as in the case of the respondent to Professor Adiga's article) of being Un-American and Un-Patriotic. Finally, we have those that detach themselves and express an attitude of "I don't have to deal with it so it's not my problem." *But* if we are all human beings, do not all these problems belong to all of us?

I don't have all the answers, but maybe a simple step that anyone who wants to improve race relations can take is to empathize. So the next time someone from a background different from yours mentions an experience that is one you have not lived, just listen, reflect, and most importantly, *empathize* before reacting and responding. Maybe empathy can help us all bond as human beings. [7]

END NOTES

[1] Gabrielson, Ryan, Ryann Grochowski Jones, and Eric Sagara. "Deadly Force, in Black and White." *ProPublica*. 14 Oct. 2014. Web. 27 May 2015.

[2] Blow, Charles M. "Hate Takes the Bus: A University of Oklahoma Fraternity's Chant and the Rigidity of Racism." *The New York Times*. 11 March 2015. Web. 27 May 2015.

[3] "White House History Timelines: African Americans: 1790s-1840s." *The White House Historical Association*. Web. 1 June 2015.

[4] "Life on the Reservations." *U.S. History: Pre-Columbian to the New Millennium*. http://www.ushistory.org/us/40d.asp. Web. 1 June 2015.

[5] "Living Conditions." *Native American Aid*. www.nrcprograms.org. Web. 1 June 2015.

[6] Bourne, Jenny. "Slavery in the United States." EH.net. Web. 1 June 2015.

[7] The author recognizes that many racial groups were not discussed in this essay. To address all groups is beyond the scope of this essay. The author hopes that readers will take the essay in the spirit in which it was written: to provoke thought and reflection on issues of race, as well as hopefully giving some ideas to promote understanding among all people.

Reflection on the Important Power of an Anthology on Race

Brother Brian Henderson, FSC
Trustee & Former Director of Saint Gabriel's Hall

Lyrics of Bruce Springsteen's song Darkness on the Edge of Town states,

> *"Everybody has a secret Sonny (a story that involves persons or people), something that they just can't face. Some folks spend their whole lives trying to keep it. They carry it with them every step that they take. Until some day, they just cut it loose, cut it loose, or let it drag them down. Where no one asks any questions or looks too long in your face."*

A lot happens to people in life without realizing or acknowledging the emotional, spiritual, or attitudinal impact. So much occurs leaving people speechless, absent words to describe or express their feelings. Social habits and norms encourage compartmentalizing feelings so to ignore, put aside, or even bury true authentic feelings. "If you don't mind, it doesn't matter." However, people do mind and it does matter. Feeling discounted, marginalized, and ignored, core driving facets of racism, are deeply personal experiences of human disconnection from dignity and respectful regard. Current norms tell people to ignore these feelings and be strong. However, in my sixteen years of working with court adjudicated youth, a disproportional percentage of them African American, many already burdened by pervasive racism, these deeply hurtful feelings become "something they can't face." Most spent their whole lives trying to keep their hurt feelings hemmed in, carrying these with them every step that they take. Deep down, these hurtful feelings turn toxic, becoming ever more painful and disruptive to a sense of grounded equilibrium.

Racism is personal. It is uprooting dignity done one-to-one, group-to-group, social systems upon the back of "the outed-crowd." It stabs at the humanness of each individual involved with its unspoken, not confronted perpetuation. People individually and collectively carry these feelings deep down where they become what I call "festering puss balls" that inevitably heat up and eat at persons who have to make a choice, "They just cut it loose, or let it drag them down." Without constructive expression, pent up heated emotions can simply cut loose and explode forth increasing parallel cycles of harmful reacting, and dug-in ignorance. Further burying even more toxic raw anger until it is untenable to carry and so a person or people might begin to die emotionally. The hard-faced teenage youngsters I worked with had seen too much, carried too much, and experienced too much harm and hurt from racism and its associative hurtful facets. All the while, told to just carry on but do not react. These unspoken festering feelings diminish solid emotional intelligence and management, inevitably contributing to impulsive, destructive reactive behaviors that ruin lives.

Fortunately, I have seen art used as a tool to change these cycles! I witnessed Art Therapy or art as therapy serve as powerful tools for saving people who emotionally died. Being emotionally dead is not allowing feelings to have voice, expression, and realization, leading to tremendous spiritual and attitudinal harm as well as a frozen brittleness of the soul. Lyrics of a hymn that honors the work of Saint John Baptist De La Salle, celebrates him as "one sent to the children, vanquisher of ignorance so deadly to the soul." Drawn and/or written art offers people initial steps toward acknowledging the shape, shades, and depth of feelings that can lead to storytelling, experience sharing. Eventually art invites conversation and conversation starts the pathway to healing, refreshing, and redeeming the warmth of the soul, becoming emotionally alive once again. Ultimately, dialogue is so necessary for acknowledging accurately the occurrence of hurt and harm so a path toward recovery from the disruption of emotional grounded equilibrium becomes possible. Art can be a compelling tool for addressing questions no one wants to ask or to look long into the face of pain and suffering. We, all of us, need to see racism on and through the face of those who withstand the worst of its devastating discounting of their humanity as individual and collective human beings.

Society faces racism poorly, if attempted at all. We fail to behold or gaze upon the devastating destructive power of such a discounting force to human dignity because it is inconvenient and easier to allow racism to remain hidden, out of sight and out of mind. Art compels our souls to act differently, first by understanding through beholding the pain, suffering, and humiliating degradation of a fellow human being. Racism is too often faced through destructive explosions of pent-up toxic emotions because the pervasively malevolent neglect, marginalization and straightforward abuse of racism goes ignored as well as persistently perpetuated as acceptable because nothing can be done about it except keep silent about it. Generation upon generation avoids racism claiming, "we have already conquered it," but only in fantasies.

I often witnessed in my work with inner-city youngsters and youngsters adjudicated as delinquent, so much of what traumatized and troubled them become locked in, creating a bubbling cauldron of toxic energy. Few, if anyone, asks them "what happened to you?" Rather people more often ask the accusatory question, "What is wrong with you?" These children have great difficulty communicating through words but art seems to give them a way for getting out some of those locked inside toxic feelings. When one paints a picture of a story or writes creative prose or poetry about an experience, the real root story of harm and hurt begins to find expression. In sharing, comes the first step toward recapturing horizons of hope.

Art often allows both adults and children to be children again and have a disposition more pure, free of the dreadful seriousness that often accompanies the lifelong hurt and harm racism gives. Art and the accompanying storytelling provide a safer pathway of revealing and letting go of the toxic nature of hurt and harm. A former colleague, Greg Ensanian, is quoted in a book by Maureen O'Connell titled *If These Walls Could Talk:* "If a kid has trouble expressing himself in words he can express these things through art. Art allows us to see symbols that then allow you to see a variety of emotional states" (117). In the same chapter, Margaret Miles observes that the object of art is "to objectify feeling so that we can contemplate and discuss it" (117). Art helps name deep-seated facets of ourselves, our humanity, and create a safe space outside of ourselves in which to engage and express those feelings. Art enhances emotional literacy and expands consciousness making it easier to read the signs of ourselves as well as those of our other selves. The dreadful and ugly art transforms into compelling and beautiful expression. Human beings fear the dreadful and ugly but in facing them, gain confidence in the light of beauty, even when that beauty expresses the most difficult felt experiences of life.

Art is a tool to combat the darkness at the edges of human emotions generated by racism that precipitate harm, hurt, and toxicity carried with every step taken. What needs facing, art can help bring into light. I have witnessed this several times, in light one begins to let go of that which threatens human goodness and then no longer allow ugly racism to have power over the goodness of diverse humanity. So let us celebrate and allow the art herein to begin and continue the work of vanquishing the ignorant harm and hurt of racism.

REFERENCES

O'Connell, Maureen H. *If These Walls Could Talk: Community Muralism and the Beauty of Justice.* Liturgical, 2012.

Bearing Witness to White Supremacy from Inside

Rosemary A. Barbera, Ph.D., MSS
Associate Professor of Social Work

"We live in an age in which silence is not only criminal but suicidal . . . for if they take you in the morning, they will be coming for us that night." James Baldwin (1970)

On 16 July, 2013 George Zimmerman was acquitted of the murder of Trayvon Martin. I remember it vividly. We were celebrating my Afro-Latino son's 8th birthday along with the arrival of some friends from Chile. The atmosphere was happy until the news came about the acquittal. The mood changed to disbelief and anger. **Bam** – *first punch in the gut*. We had all seen the news, read the stories, followed the case. How could it be that a teen paid with his life for stepping out to buy Skittles and iced tea and his murderer would walk free? It was beyond belief. And although I considered myself someone who understood racism in U.S. society, it took this white woman from Philadelphia to a different level. It forced me to dig deeper, reflect harder, and confront my own feelings and beliefs of white supremacy. I knew I had to be more proactive in better understanding how white supremacy permeates all aspects of life in the United States so that I could be a better mother and a better person in general.

After the Zimmerman verdict I jumped on the bandwagon and took a picture of myself with a hoodie to show solidarity. Then I found a webpage called "I am not Trayvon Martin." It was a powerful awakening to me. The posts on this page were mostly from white women like myself who up until now thought that their desire to undo racism helped them rid themselves of white supremacy. They, and I, now realized that it would not be so easy; that whites really cannot know what it is like to be Trayvon Martin, or his parents, or people of color in general in U.S. society. One woman articulated what I had been feeling, but could not put into words, as she wondered what would happen when her whiteness could no longer protect her Black son? **Bam** - *second punch in the gut*. I had been wondering at what age my cute son would no longer be seen as cute, but be perceived as a menace in a white supremacist society? Would it be at 17 like Trayvon Martin? Sadly, the age was much younger than 17. The answer came a little over a year later when 12-year-old Tamir Rice was shot to death by the police for playing with a toy gun in a park. **Bam** - *third punch in the gut*. Of course, these gut punches are the daily reality for people of color in the United States. They have to navigate a society that continues to treat them as second-class citizens. Sometimes this treatment is intentional. Other times this treatment is a consequence of decisions, policies, and actions on the part of individuals and government (West, 2010; see also Coates, 2015). Either way, this treatment is motivated by the white supremacy that is part of the fabric of the U.S., and part of my own history, as well.

I was born into a family of Italian descent and grew up in a white, middle class neighborhood in Philadelphia where I attended white schools. The racism, sexism, ethnocentrism, and Anti-semitism in my family were pervasive. Once I walked into my parents' home with a cap that read "Say No to Racism." My mother asked me to remove it because she was afraid the cap would upset and offend my father. True story. It never felt quite right to me. On the one hand in my religious school we were learning that all people were God's children. On the other hand at home I was learning that some people were better than others. Eddie Glaude talks about how "(W)e learn race in the places we live not as rules, but as habits – as a kind of general know-how that enables us to get about" (2016, p. 55). Our understanding of the world, and our place in it, are taught to us through the daily habits that we take part in. If that reality is racist, we learn to be racist, regardless of whether or not we want to be. As Glaude says, "Most of our habits are like this. They aren't instinctive. Instead, they are acquired in the context of a shared life with others – in our dealings with family and friends, in the particular places where we *experience* (italics added) life" (2016, p. 62). So our racial habits become normalized and we rarely stop to think about them since "(T)he reality is that we privilege people who look and act like us, and perceive those who don't as different and, frequently, inferior" (Emdin, 2016, p. 19). Unless we intentionally stop to think, time and again, about the structure of society and our place in it, we are doomed to perpetuate racism and injustice.

After high school I chose to attend college at a school located in a diverse area because I realized that my life was too sheltered and too white. While I had been taught that the United States was a free society where hard work always leads to success regardless of race or ethnicity, I saw with my own eyes people who worked very hard yet still lived in abject poverty. And those people where usually Black and Brown. Taylor (2016) asserts that "The Black experience unravels what we are supposed to know to be true about America itself – the land of milk and honey, the land where hard work makes dreams come true" (p. 25). In other words, the existence of Black and Brown people in the United States was an affront to the myth of a colorblind society where all persons enjoyed the same freedoms and the same opportunities. It was easier to claim colorblindness rather than confront the harsh, cruel, and unjust reality of white supremacy.

Recognizing that I benefit from white supremacy was not an easy realization. I began to understand the issue of white privilege, and saw how when I spoke Spanish with my husband in public we were treated differently than when we spoke English. But I still thought white supremacy was too harsh a term to explain the reality of the United States. The deaths of Trayvon

Martin, Tamir Rice, Eric Gardner, Sandra Bland, Michael Brown, and so many others – a series of gut punches - demonstrated how little #BlackLivesMatter. In a letter to his nephew, James Baldwin explained:

> (Y)ou were born into a society which spelled out with brutal clarity, and in as many ways as possible, that you were a worthless human being. You were not expected to aspire to excellence: you were expected to make peace with mediocrity. (1962, p. 7)

These words 55 years later still ring true; they keep me up at night as the mother of two Afro-Latinx children. My struggle against racism that grew out of a general concern for social, economic, and racial justice in society has become more urgent as I watch my children grow and as I wish for them the same opportunities that were available to me. I wonder – how often will I have to have "the talk" with my son and daughter?

Overcoming the habit of racism (Glaude, 2016) is not easy. It requires vigilance and awareness. I must be willing to question assumptions, to be open to criticism from people of color, and to feel uncomfortable as I continue to learn about the horrific injustices perpetrated in my name in order to maintain the status quo. I have to be willing to provoke my own gut punches. But I must not allow guilt to overcome me. Guilt can be paradoxical. On the one hand it can be overwhelming and lead to being immobilized. On the other hand it can let us off the hook because it allows us to believe that we have overcome the racism. Guilt alone will not rectify 450 years of oppression, domination, suffering, and injustice. Only following the lead of our brothers and sisters of color and taking action will do that.

As an educator I try to teach by example. I am honest and open about the biases that I still find creeping into my mind. In fact, when I have a biased thought, I immediately record it in a file I have created in my phone, and if it happens in class, I explain to students what I am doing and why I am doing it. As a person committed to being part of the struggle to build a just society I have no choice but to continue to fight against racism and white supremacy, whether it is found inside of me or in society. If we truly want to right the wrongs of past generations, then we must acknowledge how those wrongs continue to permeate our lives and our society today; how they benefit some, to the exclusion and suffering of others. We must be willing to confront white supremacy in people we know and people we may not know. It may not always make us feel good, but it is what must be done. Silence is not an option since "injustice anywhere is a threat to justice everywhere" (King, 1967, para. 4). We are all connected, but some of us have more advantages than others. We must use that advantage to prioritize justice and liberation, before they come for us at night.

REFERENCES

Baldwin, J. (1962). *The fire next time*. New York: Vintage International.

Baldwin, J. (1970). An Open Letter to My Sister, Miss Angela Davis. Retrieved from http://www.nybooks.com/articles/1971/01/07/an-open-letter-to-my-sister-miss-angela-davis/

Coates, T. (2015). *Between the world and me*. New York: Spiegel & Grau.

Emdin, C. (2016). *For white folks who teach in the hood . . . and the rest of y'all too: Reality pedagogy and urban education*. Boston: Beacon Press.

Giddings, P. (1984). *When and where I enter: The impact of Black women on race and sex in America*. New York: William Morrow.

Glaude, E. S. (2016). *Democracy in Black: How race still enslaves the American soul*. New York: Crown Publishers.

King, M.L. (1963). Letter from a Birmingham Jail. Retrieved from: https://web.cn.edu/kwheeler/documents/Letter_Birmingham_Jail.pdf

Taylor, K.Y. (2016). *From #BlacklivesMatter to Black Liberation*. Chicago: Haymarket Books.

West, C. (2010). *Democracy Now*. Retrieved from https://www.democracynow.org/2010/11/19/cornel_west_on_charles_rangel_bush

Navigating Racial Schizophrenia in an Era of Colorblindness
By Charles A. Gallagher, PhD
Professor of Sociology

Traditional age college students, some born around 2000, were raised in a climate of race relations and racial events that taken in total can only be described as schizophrenic. The formative years of most of college students had them watching, listening, and being led by a president who was black; the first African American to ever hold this office. Not only did President Barack Obama's two-term presidency create the optic that a black president was unremarkable and normal, but the cohort of students now in college grew up watching in real-time one of the President's daughters go from a cute ten-year-old girl with braces to a gifted student who is now in Harvard's graduating class of 2021. What we saw in this exceptionally close knit, loving family of four was the personification of the American Dream. The former First Lady Michelle Obama's great grandfather was a slave. President Barack Obama is the son of a black immigrant from Kenya. The former First Lady and the President respectively attended the elite universities of Princeton and Columbia undergraduates, went on to Harvard Law School and met while working at Sidley and Austin, an international prestigious Chicago law firm. The adage that "Only in America can anybody can become president" seems, at least in the specific case of Barack and Michelle Obama, true. Eight years of a black man running the executive branch of government set in motion a cultural narrative in social media, the press and among conservative opinion makers that the United States had entered into an era of colorblindness. Colorblindness "is the tendency to claim that racial equality is the norm, while simultaneously ignoring or discounting the real and ongoing ways in which institutional racism continues to disadvantage racial minorities ... and reflects the fact most whites, as expressed in national polling data, now view race as a benign social maker that has little or no bearing on an individual's or group's educational, economic or occupational mobility" (Gallagher, 2015 p. 40).

In many ways the U.S. *appears* to be moving towards colorblindness. In addition to a black president, Valerie Jarrett, Obama's Chief of Staff, was the first black to serve in that capacity and the nation saw the selection of its first black Attorney General in Eric Holder Jr. and subsequently the first black female Attorney General in Loretta Lynch. Media mogul Oprah Winfrey has a net worth of over two billion dollars, Michael Jordan is a billionaire, and super stars Beyoncé and Jay Z's combined wealth also puts them in the billionaires club. The addition of a Latina to the Supreme Court, Sonia Sotomayor, as well as the selection of other women has made the nation's highest court the most diverse in our nation's history. People of color seem to occupy positions of authority and responsibility at all levels of America's occupational hierarchy and enjoy the same civil rights and non-discriminatory treatment as whites. All these trends represent real progress in tearing down the racial barriers that excluded so many from equal rights and social mobility.

There is, however, a cruel fiction that is the flip side of this progress. The typical 20-year-old today—thanks to a 24/7 news cycle and ubiquitous social media—watched on television over and over the death, to name just a few, of Trayvon Martin, Eric Garner, Sean Bell, and Michael Brown, unarmed black men killed by the police. They have watched race riots take place in Ferguson Missouri in 2014, Baltimore Maryland in 2015, and Milwaukee Wisconsin in 2016. In 2015, 93 unarmed individuals were killed by the police, 37 of whom were black men (Lowery, 2016). College students today came of age seeing the rise of Black Lives Matter, a social protest organization that emerged to bring to public attention police brutality and other facets of systemic racism. Others see Black Lives Matter as an anti-white, anti-police officer hate group, which I believe is an extreme distortion of their mission. The result was the creation of White Lives Matter, and as their mission statement explains is an organization "dedicated to promotion of the white race and taking positive action as a united voice against issues facing our race," and Blue Lives Matters, an pro-police organization that promotes the concerns of police officers. In the 2016 presidential campaign we witnessed a bruising presidential election where President Trump demeaned immigrants from Mexico and Central America, framed all Muslims as a national security threat, and described America's inner cities (read blacks) as "disasters." On June 17, 2015 an admitted white supremacist, Dylan Roof, walked into the Emanuel African Methodist Church in Charleston, South Carolina and methodically assassinated nine African American church members taking part in a bible study. He had hoped his killing spree would start a race war.

Colorblindness is a story line told over and over in most parts of the media while race riots rage and white supremacy groups are on the rise. This is the social schizophrenia I referenced in the opening: a nation ostensibly moving towards colorblindness while racist and xenophobic acts throughout the country happen with greater frequency. The largely false premise that occupational mobility is now the same for everyone regardless of race (or gender, religion or sexual orientation) and institutionalized racism and discrimination is a practice of the past has become the new narrative of race relations in the United States. Colorblindness as a way of seeing and understanding race relations and the racial hierarchy that continues to allocate resources based on color rests on certain core beliefs that have their root in cherished American ideals.

The first rests on the belief that equal opportunity is now the norm. What this means is that race no longer affects life chances, that is, who goes to college or lands a white collar job or who is or is not subject to "stop and frisk" police programs. Race is viewed by sizable parts of the US population as no longer being a factor in how individuals treat one another. Part of this belief in equal opportunity being the norm is that the socio-economic playing field has been leveled. Where you wind up in the socio-economic hierarchy reflects a mix of hard work, grit, investments in human capital (schooling or technical training), and touch of luck; race, as it is viewed by majorities, has nothing to do with it.

This schizophrenic view that on one hand racism still infects so many parts of society and the countervailing belief that we have transcended race is evident in nationally representative polling data. Various polls taken about institutional racism, treatment by the police, quality of schools and racial attitudes suggest that whites, typically by very large margins, believe that race plays little or no role in how racial minorities are treated. A 2015 CNN poll found that 81% of whites believed blacks have as good enough chance of getting a job as whites, 43% in this poll believed most or all of the goals of the civil rights movement have been achieved and close to half (49%) of whites believed the criminal justice system treats whites and blacks equally. A Pew study in 2016 found that although a majority of whites (53%) believe that "Our country needs to continue making changes to give blacks equal rights with whites," close to four out of ten (38%) believe the country has already made the changes "to give blacks equal rights with whites." This Pew study also found that a significant amount of white Americans (41%) believe that there is "too much" attention paid to race relations in our country. An NBC poll found that a majority of whites (59%) believe people are NOT judged by the color of their skin. While much of white America has come to believe that the old style Jim Crow racism that stifled opportunity and resulted in institutional racism has significantly decreased or been eradicated, a sizable number of whites (50%) in a 2015 poll by the Public Religion Research Institute believe that "discrimination against whites is as big a problem as discrimination against blacks and other minorities."

There are then two competing narratives about how far we have come in relation to racial equality and social mobility when we look at whites and racial minorities in the United States. There is no question that by many empirical measures the socio-economic playing field has been moving towards equality. The percent of racial minorities attending college has more than doubled since 1993, but graduation rates and the percent attending college lags significantly behind whites. Four in ten blacks own their own home but the number is seven in ten for whites. In 2013 median wealth for white families was $141,900 compared to Latinos at $13,700 and blacks at $11,000 (Vega, 2016). The poverty for Blacks and Latinos is typically double that of non-Hispanic whites. Infant mortality rates are three times higher for black women compared to white women. We live in a country that is increasingly multiracial and multi ethnic but our institutions are disproportionately white. As of 2016 the non-Hispanic white population in the United States was 62%. All things being equal, that is if the playing field were truly level, we should see are major institutions staffed and controlled with numbers that reflect the US population. In other words whites should be in control of no more than 62% of the organizations and institutions that reflect power, prestige, and avenues to wealth. What we see, however, in 2016 is that whites are still vastly overrepresented in the halls of power and in the most desirable occupations; 83% of the 144th congress is white; 90% of all elected officials are white; 95% of all elected prosecutors are white; 96% of all Fortune 500 CEOs are white; 75% of all doctors are white; 87% of all college president are white; 82% of full and 75% of associate professors are white.

We are at a crossroads regarding race relations that is unlike any other in American history. There is a belief, borne out in many examples that people of color are making great strides. Compared to 100 years ago this is true. But on many social and economic fronts this progress has stalled and in some instances like school integration actually reversed. We have a vision of our nation, one that neatly conforms to deeply held conviction in equality that co-exists with systemic institutionalized racism and most recently the rise of far-right political and social movements. In 1968, the Kerner Commission issued a report trying to explain why so many cities in the 1960s exploded in violent race riots. National Advisory Commission on Civil Disorders. 1968a, b. The iconic quote generated from this commission captured what anyone who read a national newspaper, traveled in the South, or visited poor black urban neighborhoods knew: "Our nation" the report said "is moving toward two societies, one black, one white — separate and unequal." That was 50 years ago and we have taken mere baby steps in addressing this dilemma. The real problem for those under thirty is this: there was no colorblind counter narrative in the 1960s and 1970s to explain away, distract, or shift blame to racial minorities for the embedded racism in American society. While a "culture of poverty" argument emerged as an explanation of the causes of intergeneration poverty, there was no deeply help ideological belief that most of the nation shared regarding racial inequality. That is not the case today. Pending what one reads or the media outlets one listens to, one can find a story line that confirms existing beliefs (confirmation bias) but ignores the sociological and empirical reality of the causes of poverty, racial inequality, and institutional racism. There are now competing realities to explain why some groups make it and some groups don't. One typically blames the individual for lacking traits that could make them successful, or the group is inherently lazy, or a more sociological and structural explanation that understands how past exclusion of racial groups to paths of upward mobility play out today. These beliefs, failed individuals or failed structures, are communicated by our leaders. As the keynote speaker for the National Democratic Convention in 2004 then Senator Barack Obama said, "There is not a Black America and a White America and Latino America and Asian America—there's the United States of America." Although in later speeches President Obama touched on racial inequality, his pivot here was that a shared citizenship, love of country, and being an American transcended race. Compare Barack Obama's reflection with those of then presidential candidate Trump's comments on June 16, 2015. Part of candidate Trump's stump speeches involved the wholesale denigration of immigrants, many of whom are racial minorities. Donald Trump said, "When Mexico sends it people, they're not sending their best. They're not sending you. They're sending people that have lots of problems, and they're bringing those problems with us. They're bringing drugs. They're bringing crime. They're rapists. And some, I assume, are good people." An appeal to colorblindness and American citizens' better angels on one hand and racist fear mongering on the other. This is now the political reality that America's youth will have to navigate for the foreseeable future.

REFERENCES

CNN/ORC Poll. Feb. 12-15, 2015. N=1,027 adults nationwide (margin of error ą 3), including 733 non-Hispanic whites (ą 3.5), and, with an oversample, 309 blacks (ą 5.5).

Gallagher, C. (2015). Color-blind egalitarianism as the new racial norm. In K. Murji and J. Solomos (Eds.), *Theories of race and ethnicity: Contemporary debates and perspectives.* (pp. 40-56). Cambridge: Cambridge University Press.

Lowery, W. (2016, April 7). Study finds police fatally shoot unarmed black men at disproportionate rates. *Washington Post.* Retrieved from https://www.washingtonpost.com/national/study-finds-police-fatally-shoot-unarmed-black-men-at-disproportionate-rates/2016/04/06/e494563e-fa74-11e5-80e4-c381214de1a3_story.html?utm_term=.9495a028468e

National Advisory Commission on Civil Disorders. 1968a. *Report of the Commission on Civil Disorders.* New York: Dutton. (Kerner Commission Report)

National Advisory Commission on Civil Disorders. 1968b. *Supplemental Studies for The National Advisory Commission on Civil Disorders.* Washington, DC: U.S. Government Printing Office. (Kerner Commission Report)

NBC News/Wall Street Journal Survey, Hart Research Associates/Public Opinion Strategies Study #13266, July 2013.

Pew Research Center, On Views of Race and Inequality, Blacks and Whites Are Worlds Apart, June 27, 2016.

Public Religion Research Institute (PRRI), 2015. Anxiety, Nostalgia, and Mistrust, Findings from The 2015 American Values Survey.

Vega, T. (2016, June 27). Blacks still far behind whites in wealth and income. Retrieved from CNN Money website: http://money.cnn.com/2016/06/27/news/economy/racial-wealth-gap-blacks-whites/index.html

Vega, T. (2016, January 26). Why the racial wealth gap won't go away. Retrieved from CNN Money website: http://money.cnn.com/2016/01/25/news/economy/racial-wealth-gap/index.html

Diversity Management: Legal and Ethical Challenges for Aspiring Workplace Leaders

Karen A. Reardon, PhD, JD
Associate Professor of Management and Leadership

During the Johnson Administration, Congress passed the Civil Rights Act of 1964 which prohibits racial discrimination in employment based on five protected classes, including race. Fifty years later, the need for the law is as evident as ever. In 2016, the United States Equal Opportunity Employment Commission (EEOC) processed over *ninety-one thousand* claims by employees that they were subject to discrimination against, including thirty-two thousand based on race (including reverse discrimination) with an additional three thousand based on color and nearly ten thousand based on national origin. Other claims included thirty thousand based on sex, nearly four thousand based on religion and over forty-two thousand claims that employees were retaliated against for reporting misconduct (EEOC 2016 Charge Statistics). These statistics are startling given that they do not include charges of discrimination filed only at the state or local level and that most acts of discrimination never become the subject of legal claims over fear of retaliation.

Business managers and executives are entrusted with important decisions that impact individual and familial economic well-being. While we can educate the aspiring executive about discrimination laws and their legislative history, how might we communicate how hurtful and divisive race-based (and other discriminatory) employment decisions can be to those who are subject to them? Shouldn't we do so when diversity is good business? Leading business publications such as Forbes report on emerging research that shows racially diverse workforces actually outperform others (Tulshyan, 2015). So, how do we respectfully share views *and feelings* about the reality of discrimination or the impact of Affirmative Action policies? Do these laws and polices serve a valid purpose by opening doors to historically disenfranchised groups or perpetuate race-based decision making in employment? Consistent with Gilligan's Ethics of Care or Aristotle's Virtue Ethics, how do we begin to talk about these important issues one human being to another?

In some MBA classes at La Salle, we have used the Van Buskirk-London Poetry Gallery model (2012) to create space in which to have conversations about race and other important *human* issues encountered in the workplace. In the Gallery, students read poetry posted on the walls of a classroom entering as they would an art gallery with soft music playing. Each has the opportunity to experience the poetry and reflect on it from his/her vantage point as well as to share those views—first with a conversation partner and then with the class in a conversation circle. After the experience, students reflect on the experience in writing as an assignment, the text of which appears in the Teaching Notes section at the end of the Anthology. Through this exchange, students hear how persons of color bristle at the notion that they are less-deserving when others assume they achieved success because of Affirmative Action policies. The sons and daughters of contemporary immigrants and those who are themselves immigrants speak about the challenges of that status and how much they or their families have sacrificed to come to this country—documented or undocumented—and to be American. We ask if and how they are different than the waves of European immigrants of the 1800s and 1900s? In reflection on a poem about a young girl of Japanese origin subject to internment during World War II, we discover and discuss frightening similarities between that now disavowed practice and current bans on immigration from predominantly Muslim lands undergoing legal challenge. More often than not, the class emerges from sharing more appreciative of the differences between us, yet united by our common humanity.

The writings that comprise the Anthology function as windows into the lives, thoughts and feelings of the student authors. As such, they should be treated with great care and respect. Using the Van Buskirk-London model, they too could adorn classroom walls to stimulate reflection, sharing and problem solving on issues of race and others that divide or unite us. It is our hope they might help other readers imagine, understand their responsibility for and be motived to work collaboratively to build a more beloved community and world.

REFERENCES

Civil Rights Act of 1964, 42 U.S.C. Sections 2000(d) et seq.

Tulshyan, R. (2015, January 30). *Forbes*. Retrieved from https://www.forbes.com/sites/ruchikatulshyan/2015/01/30/racially-diverse-companies-outperform-industry-norms-by-30/#3273731d627d)

U. S. Equal Opportunity Employment Commission Charge Statistics. Retrieved from http://www.eeoc.gov/eeoc/statistics/enforcement/charges.cfm)

Van Buskirk, W. and London, M. (2012). Poetry as deep intelligence: A qualitative approach for the organizational behavior classroom. *Journal of Management Education, 36*, 636-668.

Racism and Health Disparities: The Role of Health Care Professionals

By Sara Shuman, PhD, MPH
Assistant Professor of Public Health

Health professional students are often surprised to learn that social determinants (i.e., wealth, education, occupation, racism, discrimination and gender) play a larger role in determining health behaviors and outcomes than biology or genetics. However, research investigating racial disparities in health across issues — from obesity to HIV to domestic violence —provides strong evidences that genetics alone do not determine health. For example, in the United States, racial minority patients receive lesser quality pain management compared to whites, regardless of the age of the patient or the type of pain management (Anderson, Green, & Payne, 2009). In other words, black children receive less/poorer quality pain management for the same condition as white children. It is important for future health care professionals to understand that disparities in health exist —but it is even more critical that they recognize that most health disparities are a result of injustice and that they must critically examine their own implicit and explicit biases to better understand how individuals, programs, and policies can be leveraged to reduce and eliminate injustice.

I volunteer in a health clinic for uninsured Spanish-speaking immigrants in Philadelphia. Recently I was interpreting for a doctor who was telling a patient in his mid-30's that the back surgery he had as a result of an occupational accident a couple of years ago was unsuccessful, and that he was never going to be pain-free or walk without a cane. That is a hard diagnosis to hear for anyone and the patient was understandably upset. What the doctor did not say was that if the patient had insurance, we would refer him to an intensive rehabilitation program where specialists could work with him to improve his gait and manage his pain, activities which would likely significantly improve his quality of life. Unfortunately, his immigration status, which is inextricably linked to his race and socio-economic status, make him virtually ineligible for health insurance in the United States. Thus, he is unable to afford the cost of intensive rehabilitation facilities. Several years ago, at the same clinic, an uninsured cancer patient was discharged from the hospital because her lack of insurance limited her treatment and palliative care options. Upon discharge, she asked the clinic to help send her home to Central America so that she could be with her family. We did and she died just a few days after arriving. Her story is covered in the HBO documentary *Clinínica de Migrantes: Life, Liberty, and the Pursuit of Happiness*. Her story is just one more example of how we treat entire populations differently based on race, ethnicity, nationality, language, and ability to pay for services. I argue that healthcare is a human right and these are examples of injustices.

The link between an anti-immigrant sentiment (based on race and nationality) and poor health outcomes is well documented — unauthorized immigrants are more likely to not make or skip doctors' appointments and they wait until they are in later stages of illness before seeking help when compared to their non-immigrant counterparts (Philbin, Flake, Hatzenbuehler & Hirsch, 2017). Given the rhetoric in the popular news media and from some politicians, is it any surprise that many immigrants fear the U.S. healthcare system?

Perhaps a more reflective question is to ask what role academic institutions and educators can play in changing the trends of injustice. Evidence indicates that student exposure is crucial, exposure not only to information and multiple viewpoints, but also and especially to individuals from diverse races, ethnicities, and countries of origin. This Anthology encourages deep learning, that which can happen when students have an opportunity to engage and reflect about *and with* diverse groups of people. Recently, I asked students in a course to spend a semester thinking about how the health of different immigrant and refugee groups in Philadelphia is influenced by their history, environment, race, and culture. To do this, I accompanied small groups of students on walking "tours" to different neighborhoods in the city. We visited churches, ate in local restaurants, and talked to community leaders. We toured the library, visited murals inspired by immigrant journeys, and stopped by local health centers. At the end of the semester, I asked students to complete written reflections of their experiences. Students commented how "surprised" they were to learn that there were immigrant neighborhoods in Philadelphia beyond Chinatown. Most students had no idea that Nepali and Vietnamese refugees and Mexican immigrants lived in South Philadelphia. Others compared our classroom experience to their own family's immigrant experiences, including the Puerto Rican experience in North Philadelphia and the Eritrean experience in Southwest Philadelphia. They recognized similarities in the importance of social support to health promotion and dramatic differences in access to services compared to the native-born (and white) population. Students reflected on how grateful they were for their families and education, talked about program and policy changes needed to improve the lives of vulnerable populations, and perhaps most encouragingly, about how they wanted to learn and see more about the city and issues surrounding health access. I am confident that the 20+ students who visited a rowhome converted into a Hindu Temple, interviewed an unauthorized immigrant in her home, and know the history of Vietnamese boat people are on their way to becoming more aware and justice-oriented professionals and citizens. This is one example of how exposing students to diverse populations and ideas can open minds and hearts. There needs to be more such opportunities.

Race is a social determinant of health, but it is not a person's race that makes them unhealthy. Racism and discrimination play a large role (Paradies, 2006). Structural and personally mediated racism result in differential access to services, differential treatment, and chronic stress among individuals and populations. In turn, this encourages people to adopt unhealthy behaviors or results in the long-term release of hormones and over-stimulation of body systems, both of which result in poor health (Myers, 2009). This is unacceptable. Healthcare professionals are on the front lines of seeing the impacts of racism and have an ethical obligation to speak out and do something about it.

REFERENCES

Anderson, K. O., Green, C. R., & Payne, R. (2009). Racial and ethnic disparities in pain: causes and consequences of unequal care. *The Journal of Pain, 10*(12), 1187-1204.

Myers, H. F. (2009). Ethnicity- and socio-economic status-related stresses in context: An integrative review and conceptual model. *Journal of Behavioral Medicine, 32.* doi:10.1007/s10865-008-9181-4.

Philbin, M. M., Flake, M., Hatzenbuehler, M. L., & Hirsch, J. S. (2017). State-level immigration and immigrant-focused policies as drivers of Latino health disparities in the United States. *Social Science & Medicine.*

Paradies, Y. (2006). A systematic review of empirical research on self-reported racism and health. *International journal of epidemiology, 35*(4), 888-901.

On Mission—Let Us Not Grow Weary in Doing What is Right

Ernest J. Miller, FSC, D Min
Vice President for Mission

> So let us not grow weary in doing what is right, for we will reap at harvest time, if we do not give up. ¹⁰ So then, whenever we have an opportunity, let us work for the good of all…. Galatians 6:9 (NRSV)

Society needs artists. The church needs artists.

In Living Color: An Anthology of Contemporary Student Writings on Race is a captivating chronicle that echoes the aesthetic nature and dramatic features resident in music and writings—this display of a public theology of hope and justice—of past and present artists, from James Baldwin and Nina Simone to Maya Angelou and Kendrick Lamar. As the legendary jazz saxophonist John Coltrane notes, "To be a musician [a writer] is really something. It goes very, very deep… When you begin to see the possibilities of music [art], you desire to do something really good for people, to help humanity free itself from its hang-ups."

In an age overloaded with disappointment and despair, fear and hatred, this volume is an eloquent spiritual expression of who these lyricists and writers are—their faith, their knowledge, their being. The convictions of these student writers underscore the numerous roles that different art forms can play in culture by shining a light on critical societal issues. The works in this collection constitute a shift towards achieving what philosopher and social critic Cornel West calls "a meaning-infused moment separate from one's everyday routine—and say let me reflect on the most fundamental question of what it means to be human." Thus, it is in the deeper meanings behind artistic revelations one is hopefully able to imagine the liberation and freedom of all those dispossessed and disinherited in society.

Collectively, this elegant collection make explicit calls for political and social engagement to alleviate the prevalence of meaninglessness, hopelessness, and lovelessness that grips our society. How, then, do these works correspond to the vision and values inherent to the mission of Lasallian education? Presenting this question, it is instructive to understand the historical context in which the distinctive Lasallian characteristics of education emerged. John Baptist De La Salle (1651-1719), Founder of the Institute of the Brothers of the Christian Schools and the Lasallian movement (1680), was disturbed by the educational and social realities facing impoverished and marginalized children in late seventeenth / early eighteenth century France. Like today, the times in which De La Salle lived were infected with and affected by social injustices that enabled his society to create or tolerate callousness or indifference towards those who were economically poor and underprivileged.

Since the time of their founding nearly four centuries ago, the Brothers of the Christian Schools have had a distinctive way of looking at life through the eyes of faith. Their characteristic fraternal communion—a horizontal relationship—is a witness to the first rule of the Brothers' life: Jesus' gospel, which permeates the schools, colleges, and myriad other educational centers in the global Lasallian educational community. From the Lasallian origins, the motivation for St. De La Salle to establish a community of teaching brothers with a preferential option for those cast aside and made vulnerable is articulated by theologian Walter Kasper's contemporary theological discourse:

> What is owed every human being on the basis of his or her dignity is personal respect, personal acceptance, and personal care. In this sense, one can understand justice as the minimal measure of love and love as the full measure of justice.

From a spiritual and theological perspective, the works in this anthology convey a basic understanding of the concept of salvation. An essential element in Lasallian spirituality, salvation bears a double meaning: having dignity and standing in this world (wholeness), and ultimately experiencing the joys of eternal life. Central to De La Salle's spiritual discernment was his "double contemplation": what God wants and the urgent needs of poor children—it is salvation, liberation. Put differently, the Lasallian vision embraces an approach to education that is humanizing and liberating. "When we speak of salvation as the mission of an educational community, we must remember that salvation means more than avoiding hell and going to heaven," states educator-theologian Brother Luke Salm, FSC. "Salvation does not begin as a religious concept; it is in the first place a human reality and a human problem" (2). Brother Alvaro Echeverria, FSC, explicitly makes this assertion: This "integral salvation . . . encompasses the whole person, all persons, but with a . . . primary option for the poor, the excluded, the abandoned and young people in search of meaning." In short, Lasallian education serves as an instrument of God's liberating salvation, to use Pope Paul VI's metaphor.

The biblical and historical signposts that frame and shape the Lasallian story and vision can be read as a complementary set of identity markers through which Lasallian education attends to the anguishes and laments, the hopes and joys accentuated by *In Living Color's* keen discourse. The Lasallian polity is challenged to think, discern, and build curricular and co-curricular processes as a contribution to the problems and questions with which we struggle in our American democratic experiment. Moving forward requires a compelling vision and ethic that unleashes the potential for the justice-oriented action that the Lasallian vision in our contemporary times desires and that we, individually and collectively, must strive to render.

If we acknowledge this task, a vital question for us to consider is, "Who is my neighbor?" as presented in the Gospel of Luke. Here, the outcome of this engagement between Jesus and a curious Jewish scholar about the Great Commandment – "You shall love the Lord, your God, with all your heart, with all your being, with all your strength, and with all your mind, and your neighbor as yourself" (Lk 10:27) – "reveals Jesus' intention to bring renewal to [the ancient Jewish] community's relationship with God, not only as an ancient tradition but as a present reality," writes Cecilia Gonzalez-Andrieu (23). Achieving this renewal of community in our present reality fractured by the fumes and odors of race—a bankrupt social construct—that *In Living Color* uncovers requires moving toward an embodiment of love "in the encounter with the otherness of the other," states Kasper. For Lasallians, the mission field of education and formation is the privileged space to strive to fulfill this demand of the gospel. As Thomas Groome puts it, the goal is to engender "a way of educating for life and for all" (14).

Semejante! This beautiful poetic word—its root means to resemble—from the Spanish lexicon gives us added language to answer the question who our neighbor might be by first turning our gaze to our own humanity, says Gonzalez-Andrieu. Then it propels us to recognize the resemblance, the radical closeness of attributes, and qualities that all human beings share. Gonzalez-Andrieu continues, "Your neighbor is close and also far, needy and also comfortable, known and also unknown. Because your neighbor is precisely every single human person" (24).

Today, the Lasallian charism and mission, carried out by Brothers and other Lasallian educators in 77 countries on six continents, is buoyed by a new dynamism with its presence in multi-cultural, multi-religious, multi-ethnic environments. Accordingly, in keeping with the living tradition of the Founder and his first Brothers, Lasallian education embraces an anthropological view of human nature that

> recognizes and dignifies every human being as being unique, unrepeatable, and educable. Discrimination based on gender, culture, religion, sexual orientation or political affiliation has no place in the Lasallian educational mission. As social beings, humans are capable of establishing meaningful relationships. As spiritual beings, they are open to transcendent reality and the search for life's meaning. (Brothers of the Christian Schools 31)

This perspective provides the stage-setting from which to interrogate the Lasallian ethic to educate in faith and to educate in justice, including the promotion of racial and cultural amity. Importantly, what is required to achieve it is faithfulness to a constant reading of the "signs of the times" in the context of the Lasallian way of proceeding.

To conclude, the works in this anthology are a mélange of societal, religious, and philosophical attitudes that unite to form a call to action and to demonstrate the idea of the power of collective voices. To prosper in this task, a bold commitment is required for the long haul. Striving for racial and social justice is a long-distance run.

REFERENCES

Brothers of the Christian Schools General Council. "Circular 461: Associated for the Lasallian Mission … An Act of Hope." Sept. 2010, https://www.lasallian.info/doc/Circular%20461.pdf. Accessed 2 June 2017.

Echeverria, Alvaro Rodriguez. "A Song of Hope for the 'Regrowth' of the Founding Charism." 45th General Chapter of the Brothers of the Christian Schools, 23 Apr. 2014, Rome, Italy. Presentation.

Gonzalez-Andrieu, Cecilia. "Who is My Neighbor?" *America: The National Catholic Review*, vol. 215, no. 14, 31 Oct. 2016, pp. 21-24, http://www.americamagazine.org/sites/default/files/issues/2016/pdfs/10-31-16web.pdf. Accessed 2 June 2017.

Groome, Thomas. *Educating for Life: A Spiritual Vision for Every Teacher and Parent*. Thomas More, 1988.

Kasper, Walter. *Mercy: The Essence of the Gospel and the Key to Human Life*. Paulist, 2014.

Salm, Luke. "Together for Mission." *AXIS: Journal of Lasallian Higher Education*, vol. 7, no. 2, 2016, axis.smumn.edu/index.php/axis/article/download/184/283. Accessed 2 June 2017.

West, Cornel. "Cornel West Keynote Speech: Lesley College Diversity Day." *The Journal of Pedagogy, Pluralism, and Practice*, vol. 1, no. 1, 1997, http://www.lesley.edu/journal-pedagogy-pluralism-practice/cornel-west/diversity-keynote/. Accessed 2 June 2017.

STUDENT WRITING UNITS

UNIT ONE

Wake Up! We Have A Problem:
It Is Pervasive And Takes Many Forms

Today, it is common to hear some people argue that racism no longer exists in the United States of America, that it was swept away by the Civil Rights movement in the 1960s, a period that ushered in a new era of tolerance and equality. Yet, many others argue that racism continues to be a divisive and even deadly problem in our country. Several of the faculty frames in this anthology make and support this latter claim through both scholarly research and personal experience. In Unit One, La Salle students explore the ongoing challenges of racism in the contemporary United States. From research papers to reflective essays to poetry, students use a variety of genres to express their ideas about just how far we still have to go in promoting racial equity in America. These readings will be useful in a variety of disciplines across the humanities and social sciences to understand our own students' perspectives about racism's continuing influence on individuals and society.

SLEEPING ON THE KING'S DREAMS

Wake Up! Wake Up!

Wake up and do, wake up and be. We've fallen asleep on the King, we have forgotten his dream.

Wake Up! Wake Up!

50 years have gone by, some progress has been made, some lives have been changed,

Some blood has been shed to keep the dream alive.

United we stood, yet somehow together we died.

Today I cry,

Wake up Wake up!

I've got dreams worth more than my sleep. I stay awake with no counts for sheep. Dreams I cast away, though nightmare I keep.

Nightmares is all that I see.

I'm from the city of brotherly love, where love is conditional, brothers aren't traditional.

They have put down their books to pick up guns.

You see, they think it's cool to run up in our schools and shoot down our kids.

Victims of Sandy Hook please rest in peace, your memories, we'll try to keep.

Forgotten symbols of hope, become the reality of a freedom eloped, gone with the wind, and with him his friends, justice, equality, respect.

If King were here he'd hang his head, not by the threads of a rope entangled in hate, but by the shame we've brought on our own sleeping race.

Wake Up! Wake Up!

I ask you, how do we dare sleep

when 47 million Americans in poverty;

when 26% Americans do not earn a living wage;

when Black men are more likely to go to prison than college in this country;

when nearly 2 million Americans are without a home;

when 26,000 foster children will age out of the system without a family, this year alone

You see these are statistics that I know too well; statistics that I will not let define me.

They said I wouldn't make it without my momma, they said I wouldn't make it without a father.

They said I'd be pregnant without a diploma and no hopes for a degree

But what they didn't know, is that I have a dream.

Yeah, sometimes it's not easy.

It's hard to study when your stomach screams louder than your thoughts.

I'm fighting a civil war between myself and I:

Do I fight for knowledge which gives me power, or do I submit my labor to quiet my hunger.

I must do whatever it takes to keep my dreams alive.

You must do whatever it takes to keep your dreams alive.

Don't let anyone define you, don't let anything stop you.

Do you hear me? I said

Wake Up, Wake Up!

You must be wide awake to dream his dream.

The King once said

"Our lives begin to end the day we become silent about things that matter."

If you have a dream, go follow it and be all that you can be.

PLEASE, let's not sleep any more, there are so many things we can do

There are so much more we can achieve, all things are possible if you believe.

According to the King,

"Life's most persistent and urgent question is, 'what are you doing for others?'"

Through helping others, we may find our true dreams.

So go out to your community lend a helping hand, open your heart and try to make a difference

We are more than the violence, we are more than poverty, we are more than untreated illness

We are more.

We can put an end to the violence, educate and employ our children, as we have done here at La Salle, as well as find cures for the incurable.

We will do it together, Black, White, Hispanic, Asian, all of God's Children.

It's time to resurrect the King's dream and act on it, we've fallen asleep too long.

We have buried a King, let's not bury his dream.

Awake, we can dream together. The time is now!!!!!!

WAKE UP! WAKE UP! WAKE UP!!!!!!!!!

By: Amanda Patterson, Class of 2014

I AM GOING TO TELL YOU A STORY
EXCERPT FROM FORKLESS ROAD:
A SPOKEN WORD MONOLOGUE SERIES

I am going to tell you my story now, not because I expect you to believe me. No, I'm going to tell you my story because it's the God's honest truth, and the truth shall set its teller free. In this case, the teller just so happens to be me. I am going to tell you my story now. No, not because I expect you to believe. Rather, I want you to see, that the system may trap my body but my mind will set me free. I am going to tell you my story now, but the narrative isn't exactly mine. I'm a pawn in a chess match as old as time. I'm the fruit of a poisonous vine planted long ago. I'm the seed 'massa' sowed in grandma's stomach. I'm the shame on grandpa's face. I am octoroon. I'm the middle passage. I'm slaves thrown overboard, and the deep sea plummet. I'm the auction block where blacks were sold by the hundreds. I'm the limbs that left when they caught blacks running. I'm the deed gone unpunished for far too long. I am going to tell you my story now. Not because I expect your commiseration. I tell you this story because someone's ancestors profited from my people's enslavement and someone's children will profit from mass incarceration, and the generations in between will consume our culture and appropriate our dreams. I am going to tell you my story now, and no, not a single damn word about the first black president, affirmative action, welfare, subsidized healthcare, section eight residents, color blindness or the race card. That's far too farfetched when we know that racism isn't just a card but the whole entire deck. It's racism, classism, sexism, terrorism, sadism, the rise of authoritarian statism and economic immobility. It's white universities in proximity to the ghetto. It's gentrification, assimilation, and cultural genocide in the making. It's flash mobs, rioting, looting, shooting and breaking everything we get our hands upon because we have nothing to lose. It's the dehumanization of black men and women in the news. It's white lies and selective truth. I am going to tell you my story now. Turn down your stereotypes and listen to the story of a black boy caught in the system, between a web of choiceless choices and the pipeline to prison. I'm going to tell you my story now. Shut your mouth and listen!

By: Youssef Kromah, Class of 2015

Note: The pieces in this collection were written to be read aloud, not silently.

WHY MENTAL HEALTH COUNSELORS MUST CHALLENGE ISLAMOPHOBIA

In the days and years following the attacks of September 11th, 2001, Muslims in the West have faced heightened challenges amidst stereotyping, misconceptions, racial profiling, vilification in the media, hate crimes, and discriminatory acts. Although there are an estimated 1.3 billion Muslims in the world, manifestations of anti-Islamic and anti-Muslim bigotry, referred to as "Islamophobia," continue to rise in the U.S. and other western countries (Esposito & Mogahed, 2007). In 2011, the Associated Press and other journalists exposed alarming NYPD documents that detailed spying programs that put Muslim neighborhoods, mosques, and schools under surveillance. Upon learning that informants were being recruited and that undercover officers were infiltrating their communities, a pervasive sense of anxiety, self-censorship, and mistrust of the police arose among many Muslims in the U.S. (Shamas & Arastu, 2013). In light of increasing Islamophobic sentiment, policies, and incidents, including the recent murders of three Muslim students in Chapel Hill, North Carolina, and the murder of a Muslim teen in Kansas City, Missouri, the rights, safety, and well-being of Muslims are a serious concern for mental health professionals. As stated by Haque and Kamil (2012), studies have found Muslims reporting "decreased self-esteem and increased psychological stress post 9/11" as a result of Islamophobia, therefore making it crucial for mental health professionals to "explore and understand the social, cultural, and political context of Muslim clients." Furthermore, it is critical for clinicians to become advocates for Muslim communities. Specifically, mental health professionals need to educate themselves with basic knowledge about Islam, participate in outreach work to build trust and alliances, and be active in causes that challenge Islamophobia. While there are certainly many ways counselors can advocate on behalf of Muslims, (1) education, (2) outreach, and (3) anti-racist activism will be focused upon in this paper.

There are many reasons why advocating for the Muslim community is important. While estimates about the Muslim population in America varies since the U.S. consensus does not collect religious data, the Council on American-Islamic Relations (CAIR) estimates that 6-7 million Muslims live in the United States (2012). Yet, despite their population growth, Muslims and their religion are often misunderstood and misperceived by many Americans. Nearly half (47%) of 715 American respondents of a Cornell University public opinion survey agreed that Islam is more likely to encourage violence than other religions, while an alarming 65% among highly religious respondents concurred (Nisbet & Shanahan, 2004). In a 2006 USA Today/Gallup poll,

44% of Americans stated that "Muslims are too extreme in their religious beliefs" (Esposito & Mogahed, 2007). A Washington Post-ABC News poll in 2009 found that nearly half, 48%, of American respondents said that they "have an unfavorable view of Islam, the highest in polls since late 2001."

Further unsettling are the increasing number of hate crimes and discriminatory acts committed against Muslims. Although national statistics compiled by the FBI are known to "vastly understate" the number of hate crimes (Southern Poverty Law Center [SPLC], 2012), the FBI reported that anti-Muslim hate crimes "soared by 50% in 2010, skyrocketing over 2009 levels" and marking the "highest level of anti-Muslim hate crimes since 2001." The majority of complaints about discrimination came from the workplace, while a substantial number of complaints were related to bullying in school, airport security, and profiling from law enforcement (CAIR, 2013). It is important to emphasize that discrimination and violence towards Muslims also affect communities that are mistaken or perceived as Muslims, such as Sikhs, Hindus, and Arab Christians (Kincheloe, Steinberg, & Stonebanks, 2010). The 2012 attack on a Sikh Gurdwara in Wisconsin, which left six people murdered, represents just one of many tragic incidents where the victims were mistaken for being Muslim. Within eleven days of the Gurdwara massacre, seven mosques were vandalized and attacked, including a mosque in Joplin, Missouri, which was burned to the ground (Kolsy, 2012). A Columbia University study in 2008 found that seven percent of Muslim students in New York were assaulted. To put this into perspective, there are 100,000 Muslim students in New York public schools, which means an estimated 7,000 of them have been harassed in some form. As stated by Mujahid (2008), many discriminatory acts and crimes against Muslims go unreported "as most Muslims don't trust police and the FBI enough to report them, especially considering that the FBI has knocked on the doors of 700,000 Muslim homes." The combination of negative sentiments, anti-Muslim hate crimes, and surveillance may contribute to why Muslims are often suspicious of mental health professionals. For non-Muslim clinicians, one of the ways to overcome the challenge of distrust is through educating oneself about the basics of Islam and the Muslim community (Haque & Kamil, 2012).

Due to lack of knowledge about the beliefs and values of religious groups, there is an increasing need for mental health professionals to enhance awareness about religion and spirituality in general. Previous studies have shown that many religious clients found strength in their spirituality to face problems and struggles (Sermabeikian, 1994). With regard to Islam, many non-Muslims have "very little knowledge about the religions and its followers" (Pew, 2007). Since previous studies have shown many Muslim clients citing Islam and family as major sources of strength (Hallak & Quina, 2004), acquiring basic knowledge about the religion and the Muslim community at large will significantly strengthen the therapeutic relationship (Haque & Kamil, 2012). It is important for mental health professionals to recognize the vast diversity existing within Islam and among Muslims. For instance, diversity in Islam not only exists with regard to various religious sects and different interpretations of the Qur'an, but also in reference to different racial and ethnic groups. According to Gallup's report, "Muslim Americans: A National Portrait" (2009), Muslims represent the most racially diverse religious group in the United States, with African-Americans making up the largest percentage (35%) within the population. The way in which Pakistani Muslims, for example, practice Islam may be significantly different than the way Indonesian Muslims practice the faith due to various cultural practices and traditions. Although common core beliefs bridge Muslim communities around the world, it is critical for counselors and other mental health professionals to understand the enormous complexity among diverse Muslim populations. Additionally, due to the amount of misinformation about Islam in mainstream society, clinicians should be aware of the impact these misconceptions and stereotypes have on the psychological well-being of Muslims.

Clinicians must also realize that religious adherence among Muslims ranges on various levels just like other religions. For example, a client may self-identify as Muslim, but may not feel closely connected with faith or spirituality. As stated by Haque and Kamil (2012), knowledge of Islam and the Muslim community can "bring to the forefront any biases a practitioner may have and decrease the negative impact of transference or counter transference." Another benefit of education will allow counselors to utilize historical knowledge, theology, and faith-based healing practices that communicate to the needs of Muslim clients. For example, knowledge about Islam's "long and deep legacy" in psychology and the historical contributions to the field from prominent Muslim psychologists, such as Abu Zaid al-Balkhi, al-Razi, and ibn Sina, may help clinicians working with Muslim clients who are resistant to therapy and counseling (Haque, 2004). As mental health professionals educate themselves more about Islam, engaging with the Muslim community, especially in outreach efforts, becomes equally important.

Outreach is an important component of advocacy because it allows mental health practitioners to actively engage and participate with the Muslim community. The main strengths of outreach efforts consist of developing alliances, dispelling stereotypes, building trust, and listening and learning about the legitimate concerns of the Muslim community. Rather than solely reading about Islam and Muslims, it is important for clinicians to visit mosques on interfaith events, contact religious leaders for inquiries regarding mental health issues, and organize collaborative workshops that educate Muslims about counseling services. An example of how effective outreach work can be, Chung and Bemak (2012) cite a case study of a Somali Muslim woman who struggled with lack of sleep, nightmares, and inability to concentrate at work. During the counseling sessions, the counselor learned how important Islam was to the client's identity, lifestyle, and well-being. With the permission of the client, the counselor contacted a traditional healer from the client's mosque. Together, the Muslim healer and non-Muslim therapist worked collaboratively to ease the emotional distress of the client. In other examples of case studies, counselors worked with Muslim clerics, learned about the Qur'an, and later used Qur'anic verses in therapy sessions with Muslim clients.

In whatever manner one reaches out to the Muslim community, it is "critical that it is done with honesty and authenticity, with an aim toward understanding and accepting another culture" (Chung & Bemak, 2012). However, in wake of the recent NYPD surveillance program, non-Muslim clinicians in particular need to be aware that outreach work with the Muslim community may not be an easy task. Linda Sarsour, the coordinator of the Muslim American Civil Liberties Coalition, said in response to the spying program, "We've been talking about [NYPD spying] as a civil rights issue and as a constitutional issue without understanding that this is [also] about human beings, their religious institutions, and about students chilled on their campuses" (Wessler, 2013). Soheed Amin, a recent graduate from Brooklyn College and former president of the Muslim Student Association, told the press that "at least one police informant had joined his student group and another infiltrated his mosque." He also said, "From my own experience, it ruins your life to be suspicious of everyone around you." As distrust of non-Muslims rises, mental health professionals face the challenge of overcoming this barrier. The consequences of distrust are unsettling, but one of the ways non-Muslim counselors can build trust is through social justice and anti-racist activism, specifically joining Muslims in causes that condemn and speak out against Islamophobia. In other words, it is important to go beyond simply learning about Islam, but also understanding what Islamophobia is and how it affects Muslims.

As defined by Mohideen and Mohideen (2008), Islamophobia is "the practice of prejudice against Islam and the demonization and dehumanization of Muslims. This is generally manifested in negative attitudes, discrimination, physical harassment and vilification in the media" (p. 73). One of the many dangers of Islamophobia is reflected in how society does not acknowledge it as a real social problem. Much like conversations and media coverage on racism, if Islamophobia is ever mentioned, it is often downplayed or dismissed as "isolated incidents." As a Pakistani Muslim who grew up in the United States, I have had countless experiences with Islamophobia and racism in their various covert and overt forms. There have been times when I have been called "terrorist" and "Osama" by random people based on the way I look. There also have been times when people asked me absurd questions like, "Do you support Osama bin Laden?" or "Why does your religion tell you to kill Christians and Jews?" There was one time I was at the post office and a white man randomly asked me, "Are you Indian or Paki?" When I said, "I'm Pakistani," emphasizing on the correct term ("Paki" is a racial slur), his smile faded into a frown and he said, angrily, "Shame on you." Yet when I and other Muslims share our experiences, we are often met with a lot of denial and resistance. One of the most common responses we get is, "Islamophobia isn't racist because Islam is not a race" (or "Muslims aren't a race, so they can't be victims of racism"). Muslims know full well that Islam is a religion that is open to people of all racial backgrounds. However, what is also true is how Islam has become racialized by the ideology of white supremacy, which means Muslims are cast as "threatening racial Others." The key word here is racialization, where racial characteristics and racist attitudes are assigned to groups and religions that are not races. Indeed, Islam and Muslims are not races, but they are constructed as races and the manner in which they are demonized is a heavily racialized process.

In her book, Casting Out: The Eviction of Muslims from Western Law and Politics, Sherene Razack describes the process of race thinking, which is a "structure of thought that divides up the world between the deserving and the undeserving according to descent" (2008). Within the context of Muslims in the U.S., Canada, and other western countries, Razack explains that race thinking is articulated when presidents and prime ministers of these nations talk of the "American values" or "Canadian values" they are defending in the "war on terror." Reinforced in this narrative is the notion of "culture clash," which emphasizes cultural differences between "the European majority and the Third World peoples (Muslims in particular)." Since "culture clash" focuses on cultural difference and racism, western nations declare the "superiority of European culture," by triggering stereotypical associations with Muslim-majority countries (Razack uses "the veil, female genital mutilation, arranged marriages" as examples of these associations). Reproducing this duality of "us versus them" where "the West has values and modernity and the non-West has culture," Muslims are easily marked as racial Others that are "antithetical" and "inherently opposite" to the west. We see this sharp contrast in western mainstream media depictions of Islam and Muslims, including in popular television shows like "24" and "Homeland," or in critically acclaimed films like Zero Dark Thirty and American Sniper. Muslim men are consistently portrayed as dangerous brown-skinned and bearded men holding assault rifles, rioting in the streets, burning American flags, threatening the destruction of western civilization, etc. Through this same lens, Muslim women are seen as veiled, oppressed, and sometimes dangerous, but also as victimized people that need to be rescued by western imperialism. Through this racialization process, racism surfaces to demonize Islam and Muslims and treats them as "threats."

To gain a better understanding of how Islamophobia is a form of racism, I will share an experience I had during my undergraduate years at Penn State Abington. I was one of two guest speakers for an event on Islamophobia in the West. When students were asked to write down the first thing that came to mind when they heard the words "Muslim man," the responses were consistent with the racialization I discussed above. Non-Muslim students, most of them white, wrote the following: "Arabic," "turban," "Middle Eastern," "dark-skinned," "beard," "violent," "aggressive," "controlling," "prayer rug," "terrorist," etc. When they were given the same instructions for the words "Muslim woman," they answered: "Veiled," "headscarf," "oppressed," "brown," "shy," "obedient," "religious," "serious," "exotic," etc. What became clear from the responses was that non-Muslims associated Muslim men and women not only with racialized stereotypes, but also gendered stereotypes (Muslim men were described as "controlling," while Muslim women were thought to be "oppressed," "shy," and "obedient"). When some students told me later that they didn't think my use of the word "racism" was appropriate, I reminded them of the racial characteristics they assigned to Muslim men and women. I also mentioned how Sikhs are perceived to be Muslim due to way "Muslim" is perceived to be a race. Later in the discussion, one factor that came up considerably was the media's influence on perpetuating these ideas about Muslims and Islam. In their study on the effects of microaggressions against Muslim-Americans, Nadal et al. (2012) noted how Muslim participants cited the media as having a negative impact on how they are treated and perceived. The authors wrote, "Because Islamophobic stereotypes are often viewed as acceptable in the media, it is important for educators to combat these prejudices by teaching young people about equality and acceptance." Furthermore, the researchers argued that leaders in school systems and other institutions must be mindful about the ways Muslim youth are "discriminated against, both blatantly and subtly, and how such messages impact their identities and development." In fact, after the murders of Deah Barakat, Yusor Abu-Salha, and Razan Abu-Salha in Chapel Hill, North Carolina, the sister of Deah, Suzanne Barakat, appeared on CNN and stated:

[I]t's currently an open season, a time where it's an open season against Islam, Muslims in Washington, Muslims in the general media dehumanizing Muslims in movies like American Sniper... Had roles been reversed, and no one is talking about this, but had roles been reversed and the man was Muslim, was of Arab descent, was of South Asian descent, this would have immediately been labeled an act of terror. I haven't heard anyone use the term 'terrorist' here... Why the double standard? He has terrorized our families, he has terrorized our lives, he has terrorized our community, locally, nationally, and internationally and it's time that people call it for what it is.

Yet the media continued to treat the murders in Chapel Hill as an "isolated incident," and did not connect it the larger structures of racism and Islamophobia in society. For the mental health field, where we emphasize the well being of people, it is our responsibility as advocates to not only educate ourselves about religions and cultures that are different than our own, but also listen to the people we are seeking to help and challenge injustice whenever we see it.

Social justice advocacy in the mental health profession has been growing, but there are still many contributions and efforts that need to be made. Chung and Bemak (2012) contend that social justice and human rights means to not only work with clients to "promote psychological health and wellness," but also to address "much broader political issues that impact clients' lives," such as racism, sexism, classism, and other forms of oppression. Chung and Bemak also state that "individual counseling and psychotherapy has taken passive and often insidious roles by focusing on changing the individual at the expense of changing the larger systems." The danger of overlooking systematic oppression, they argue, is "perpetuation and implicit condoning of the status quo, which historically maintains unfair and unequal power," along with reinforcing social injustices. Equally important is for counselors to engage in self-critique and be mindful of their own biases and stereotypes, particularly about marginalized communities like Muslims and people of color. According to Nadal et al. (2012), if biases are unchecked, "these stereotypes may unintentionally manifest in psychotherapy" and have negative consequences for the client.

In conclusion, the ongoing rise of Islamophobia in the United States is an urgent call for mental health professionals to recognize the importance of advocating on behalf of Muslim communities. As counselors work with more Muslim clients, the need to understand their social, cultural, and political context is greater than ever. Emphasis in this paper focused on the importance for clinicians to obtain knowledge and educate themselves about Muslims, participate in outreach programs to build better relations with the community, and to actively engage in social justice efforts that challenge Islamophobia. Learning about the effects

Islamophobia has upon Muslim individuals and families will help mental health professionals recognize the importance of social justice and advocacy work. Finally, by challenging larger and systematic forces of oppression in our society, we will not only help individuals through their struggles, but also help work towards a more compassionate, healthier, and just society for all people.

By: Jehanzeb Dar

REFERENCES

(2009) Gallup Report: Muslim Americans: A National Portrait. Retrieved from: http://www.gallup.com/poll/116260/muslim-americans-exemplify-diversity-potential.aspx

Chung, R. C.-Y., & Bemak, F. P. (2012). Social Justice Counseling: The Next Steps Beyond Multiculturalism. Los Angeles: SAGE Publications, Inc.

Esposito, J. L., & Mogahed, D. (2007). Who speaks for Islam?: What a billion Muslims really think. New York, NY: Gallup Press.

Hallak, M., & Quina, K. (2004). In the Shadow of the Twin Towers: Muslim Immigrant Women. Sex Roles. 31, 329-338.

Haque, A. (2004). Psychology from an Islamic perspective: Contributions of early Muslim scholars to psychology and the challenges to contemporary Muslim psychologists. Journal of Religion and Health, 43 (4), 367–387.

Haque, A., Kamil, N. (2012). Islam, Muslims, and Mental Health. In Ahmed, S., & Amer, M. M. (Eds.), Counseling Muslims. New York: Routledge Taylor and Francis Group.

Kincheloe, J.L., Steinberg, S.R., & Stonebanks, C.D. (Eds.). (2010). Teaching Against Islamophobia. New York: Peter Lang Publishing.

Kolsy, U. (2012). Eight attacks, 11 days. Retrieved from http://www.salon.com/2012/08/14/eight_attacks_11_days/

Mohideen, H., & Mohideen, S. (2008). The language of Islamophobia in Internet. Intellectual Discourse, 16(1), 73-87.

Nadal, K. L., Griffin, K. E., Hamit, S., Leon, J., Tobio, M., & Rivera, D. P. (2012). Subtle and Overt Forms of Islamophobia: Microaggressions toward Muslim Americans. Journal of Muslim Mental Health, 6(2), 16-37.

Nisbet, E. C., & Shanahan, J. (2004). MSRG Special Report: Restrictions on Civil Liberties, Views of Islam, & Muslim Americans. The Media & Society Research Group, Cornell University.

Pew Research Center (2007). Muslim Americans: Middle class and mostly mainstream. Retrived from: www.pewresearch.org.

Razack, S. (2008). Casting Out: The Eviction of Muslims from Western Law and Politics. Toronto: University of Toronto Press.

Shamas, D., & Arastu, N. (2013). Mapping Muslims: NYPD Spying and Its Impact on American Muslims. Long Island City, NY. Retrieved from http://www.law.cuny.edu/academics/clinics/immigration/clear/Mapping-Muslims.pdf

THIS IS OUR VOICE

Collaborators Bryan King and Derek Marshall produced a video submission for In Living Color, which you can access at https://youtu.be/4bPoXbKP1Zs. The video juxtaposes close-ups of King and Marshall's fellow students at La Salle with a poem by Marshall. We have provided a transcript of the poem below, but for the full effect, we recommended viewing the video online.

[heartbeats, followed by an anguished SCREAM]

We live in a world where governments put revenues before residents

And the only thing they bow down for is the greenbacks of their presidents

In America, where corporations are people

They knock crosses off the tops of churches and put dollar bills on steeples

And every day is a power struggle between the government and the people

The lower classes walking on glass

Hoping for a change so the struggle won't last

The media keeps deceiving us to cause divisions among the people

Tell us this race is better than that race

But all our suffering is equal

This is OUR Voice

And we're using it to take back our freedom.

[breathing and heartbeats]

By: Bryan King and Derek Marshall

THE INCREASING INCOME GAP

The United States has gone from being a comparatively egalitarian society to one of the most unequal democracies in the world, which ultimately fosters social inequality. Social inequality is characterized by the existence of unequal opportunities and rewards of different social positions or statuses within a group or society. In America inequality has always been embedded within our society and it continues to expand. These invisible social problems are continuously being ignored and they unfortunately affect individual's life chances. One of the biggest indicators of social inequality in America is the increasing wealth gap between African Americans and Caucasians.

From the beginning of the Civil Rights Movements, African-Americans were given the chance to try and mount the uphill curve of income inequality between themselves and Caucasians. Even though this movement brought about a lot of change in America, inequality amongst African-Americans and Caucasians still exists. There is not only one factor such as education, which contributes to the widening income inequality gap. Instead it would benefit this case study more effectively, if one were to look at income disparity from a multi-faceted perspective. There are three factors that are important to list as main causes of this problem.

First, the most apparent reason behind this disparity is a historical one. African-Americans have transitioned historically from being slaves to second-class citizens to first class citizens. The entrenched African American history is filled with invasions, genocide, theft, slavery, and other forms of unjust acquisitions and transfers of wealth. African Americans worked long, hard, gruesome days for centuries and they were never paid. Randall Robinson, an African American lawyer, believes that the effects of slavery produced a negative effect on African Americans. He concluded that "no nation can enslave a race of people for hundred of years, set them free bedraggled and penniless, put them without assistance in a hostile environment, against privileged victimizers, and then reasonably expect the gap between the heirs of the groups to narrow. Lines, begun parallel and left alone, can never touch" (Robinson, pg. 141). Robinson was correct in his statement since degradation did not end with slavery. Shortly after the Civil War, Black Codes were passed in former slave-holding states, these codes instituted peonage, a form of labor contract for blacks that was a little better than slavery. Former slaves had little choice but to work under these conditions because being absent from work resulted in being arrested and imprisoned. The Black Codes still promoted low wages for African Americans and it contributed to the discrimination, which can be seen throughout the Jim Crow era. The Jim Crow laws were ordinances established between 1874 and 1964 that justified the separation of whites and black races in the South of America. These laws condemned black citizens to inferior treatment and facilities. From education to public facilities, blacks were always separated from the white, which promoted the oppression of African Americans. These transitions in history allows one to speculate that because of coming from a suppressed heritage, African American levels of income potential were menial, job opportunities were low skilled and labor based, and educational attainment historically was rare since wealth was unattainable during these suppressive periods. If one starts this analysis from the implementation of the 1964 Civil Rights Act to the present, one would find that African-Americans were gradually being hired in a wider array of job sectors. In effect the income levels rose but these income increases were not significant enough for African-Americans to buy their own homes at a comparable rate to their white counterparts or attend expensive colleges.

Lower income levels generally correlate to a lower education. Education is the key to escaping lower levels of income. Since African-Americans do not have as much disposable income as whites do, their potential of educational attainment is significantly lower. Whites have an established wealth base while African-Americans suffer due to their historical circumstances. According to the US Census Bureau, the 2012 median income for white households was $57,009 and for black households it was $33.321. Even though every individual has the right to an education, the educational system in America is still unequal. Depending on the location of a public school, individuals can either receive a high-valued education or one that is not so good, due the amount of income tax a school receives. A school that receives a higher income tax generally has better access to technology, educators, and outside resources that help the students expand their knowledge, whereas a school with a lower budget has a hard time giving their students all the resources that they need. With this being said, individuals who believe that their schooling system is not top-notch are able to send their students to private schools, where they will be able to receive the best education. This unequal opportunity does not create equilibrium for education between whites and blacks. Whites have a much higher income than blacks, which explains why private schools are predominantly white students and poor-public schools are mostly black students. This notion also correlates to higher education, where white families are able to send their children to better colleges, whereas blacks have a hard time affording expensive colleges for their children. Whites generally have a significant higher level of bachelor's degrees, masters, and doctorates than African-Americans and whites can assimilate into the professional service industry that dominates America's economy at 80% according to the "CIA World Factbook." The unequal income between whites and blacks affects the future of many black students' education, contributing to the increasing wealth gap.

Since African-Americans cannot assimilate well into the workforce it produces racial discrimination in employment. Many African Americans take upon "blue-collared" professions rather than going into service-based professions. Even though the policy of affirmative action is implemented within our system, it cannot fully take away the discrimination towards African Americans. Discrimination can often cause unemployment for many African Americans due to the challenges they must overcome. For example, according to the Bureau of Labor Statistics on average the African-American unemployment rate during the month of August in the year 2013 was 13 percent while the Caucasian unemployment rate was at 6 percent. This directly shows that African Americans cannot cut through barriers in order to overcome the negativity they face in the workplace. African-Americans have a less likely chance of being hired, trained, or promoted in contrast to their white counterparts. It is possible that white business owners may feel less comfortable hiring African-Americans and would rather hire those from their own race who they feel might do a better job anyway. White Americans have negative perceptions and stereotypical biases of African-American workers, which precipitate and fuel employment discrimination. Unfortunately, racism is now an embedded transparent trait in American culture, which in relation to job employment could explain why African-Americans are twice as likely to be unemployed than their white counterparts of similar educational background.

In contrast to these arguments, one could suggest that the income disparity between African-Americans and Caucasians is not currently caused by historical implications, unequal education, or racism but the inherent problem of incarceration levels within the African-American population. There are approximately 41,000,000 million African-Americans in the United States and the percentage of this ethnic group in America that is incarcerated is 60 percent. 1 in every 15 African-American men is incarcerated in comparison to 1 in every 106 white men. Hence, one could argue that the recurring theme of incarcerations amongst African-Americans is a major hindrance to the populations' growth as a whole in terms of overall earning potentials, since there is a significant part of this population that is basically inactive due to incarceration. The inactivity of African-Americans due to incarceration is compounded with the stigma of felonies, which would not allow an individual to get a good job with a good salary. Through mass imprisonment of individuals of color, these individuals have experienced an adverse impact on themselves and on their communities from barriers to reintegrating into society, which fosters the increasing income gap.

In conclusion, social inequality is entrenched in America. The increasing wealth gap between African-Americans and Caucasians greatly affects these two group's life chances. The historical aspect is important to reflect on and illustrates the disparity between white families in America and African-

Americans in America, the latter being oppressed for centuries while the former was given the same amount of time to flourish and build a financial foothold in the emerging American society. This in turn directly correlates with entrenched lower income levels of African-Americans. Lastly, racial discrimination continues to stratify African-American job outlook opportunities while in terms of race, their white counterparts probably do not even think of job discrimination since they are a majority and may think it is a social norm for whites to be employed in better, higher positions that African-Americans. Overall, the increasing wealth gap is a social problem that needs to be changed within our society.

By: Libera Mancino, Class of 2016

REFERENCES

BLS. "Household Data." The Employment Situation- August 2013. N.p., Aug. 2013. Web. 7 Oct. 2013.
<http://www.bls.gov/news.release/pdf/empsit.pdf>.

Census Bureau. "Median Income Between Races." US Census Bureau. N.p., Jan. 2012. Web. 5 Oct. 2013. <http://www.census.gov/prod/2013pubs/p60-245.pdf>.

"Central Intelligence Agency." The World Factbook. N.p., 2012. Web. 15 Oct. 2013.

Kerby, Sophia. "The Top 10 Most Startling Facts About People of Color and Criminal Justice in the United States." The Top 10 Most Startling Facts About People of Color and Criminal Justice in the United States. Center for American Progress, 13 Mar. 2012. Web. 8 Oct. 2013.
<http://www.americanprogress.org/issues/race/news/2012/03/13/11351/the-top-10-most-startling-facts-about-people-of-color-and-criminal-justice-in-the-united-states/>.

Wenz, Peter S. "Libertarianism and Property Rights." Political Philosophies in Moral Conflict. Boston: McGraw-Hill, 2007. 122-52. Print.

CRITICAL THEORY ON RACE AND CRIME

The connection between race and crime is a very popular issue evaluated and analyzed using contemporary victimization data and statistics. Throughout the years many scholars and researchers have constructed certain theories and arguments in order to build explanations for patterns of race and crime. These theories come in many different forms and can be empirically tested to explain how two or more factors relate to one another. After reviewing the many theoretical theories that explain race and crime, the critical race theory is best to explain the relationship between race and crime. This paper will give an overview of the critical race theory and explain why this theory is related to race and crime. Furthermore, through providing evidence of race relations, racial disparities, and victimization rates, one can conclude how the critical race theory applies to the race and crime debate.

The contemporary critical race theory focuses on the fact that law maintains White supremacy. Critical race theories arose from the critical legal studies movement during the 1970s. CRT was founded by Derrick Bell, Richard Delgado and other scholars of legal studies and consist of two main goals (Gabbidon & Greene, 2005). The first goal is to understand how the law is used to maintain White supremacy and continue to oppress people of color. The second is countering or stopping these laws in order to prevent or hinder the continuation of such White supremacy. In CRT there are common perspectives which contribute to this form of white power and minority oppression. This includes the notion that racism is a norm in American society and a fact of daily life (Gabbidon & Greene, 2005). Hylton presents critical race theory as "A framework from which to explore and examine the racism in society that privileges whiteness as it disadvantages others because of their blackness and acknowledges the value of the black voice that is often marginalized in the mainstream theory, policy, and practice" (p. 224). "A Primer on Race Theory" states that assumptions of white superiority are so ingrained in political and legal structures that it becomes unrecognizable and that racial acts are reflections of larger, structural, and institutional white dominance (Taylor, 1998). This form of normalization of race both from Hylton and Taylor makes it hard to pinpoint oppression from whites because it is so instilled in their everyday thoughts and practices. Other tenets include "interest convergence" or the notion that whites benefit from racism, race as socially constructed, and that racial minorities have a unique voice in society from their distinct histories and experiences (Gabbidon & Greene, 2005). Interest convergence is a main theme of CRT constructed by Derrick Bell who argues that no civil rights legislation moves forward unless its proponents serve whites (Ladson-Billings, 2012). The unique voice of minorities in CRT is emphasized through storytelling. CRT stories inform researchers about the minorities' social reality such as oppression and victimization. These stories humanize and are direct evidence of their experiences and open the eyes of the majority (Adalberto, 2000). Although the critical race theory may be seen as unscientific due to its lack of objectives it is still a standard legal theory and is a foundation for the studies of instilled racism in civil rights laws (Gabbidon & Greene, 2005).

Critical race theory researchers focus on many aspects of socialization and socioeconomic opportunity to define its argument. Research that incorporates critical race theories examines the roles of racialized systems in shaping family structures, processes, and life chances (Buckelew & Burton, 2010). Research also shows a role of whites in a racialization system where high levels of discrimination still exist. In fact, Bobo and Charles reported that between half and three-quarters of Whites in the U.S still express negative stereotyping of minorities (Bobo & Charles, 2009).

The development of race relations article "The Perpetuation of Residential Racial Segregation in America" is direct evidence which supports the critical race theory. This article is very essential in order to argue in favor of the critical race theory because in many overt instances "interest convergence" as well as laws maintaining White supremacy are noted. This article by Marc Seitles (1996) focuses on governmental and residential segregation laws which contribute to racial ghettos, lack of affordable housing in safe suburban communities, and racial segregation. On page 1, Seitles states that public improvement projects, redevelopment projects, public housing programs, and urban renewal policies accomplish racial segregation. In fact segregation zoning ordinances are common methods to legally enforce this form of discrimination against race and income. The famous New Jersey Mount Laurel decision explains exclusionary zoning practices where local zoning was used to maintain enclaves of affluence or social homogeneity. In this, governments used this to zone out unwanted housing without having to pay anything. This form of zoning is a legal structure which preserves racial segregation and excludes the poor and minorities as well as their needs to nurture and maintain the growth of suburban communities (Seitles, 1996, p 4). Even Buckelew and Burton emphasized that "geography, namely, residential segregation, influenced the socioeconomic mobility of families" (448). These neighborhoods limited people's access to job opportunities, high quality schools, and economical advances (Buckelew & Burton, 2010).

Zoning and segregation is definitely a direct link to the critical race theory because it is "interest convergence" within itself. Zoning benefits whites in the way that they zone out minorities to keep the well being and homogeneity of suburban areas. Zoning keeps out minorities and limits the construction of affordable housing in safe neighborhoods which in turn excludes minorities from educational and employment opportunities in these areas (Seitles, 1996, p. 4). Minorities that are forced to live in areas that do not have employment opportunities or educational resources then they are forced to result to criminal behaviors. They do not have the necessary resources to go to school and learn the values of law abiding citizens nor do they higher their IQ in order to get better jobs. Almost like a domino effect. Minorities are first zoned out of good neighborhoods, which in turn zones them out of good schooling, which in turn zones them out of good jobs, which in turn leaves them in poverty, which in turn then leads to crime.

Another form of governmental policies is the Department of Housing and Urban Development or HUD which allows intentional discrimination and overt racial policies in housing procedures. Policies and practices of these agencies have let to segregation of minority communities on national and local levels. A common policy example for instance is found in the implementation of Section Eight Housing Assistance. Tenants argued that Section Eight steered minorities into apartments in segregated and crime infested neighborhoods. They also alleged that they were improperly informed of the use of subsidies in other neighborhoods and lack of information of available rent exceptions as well as the limited ability to move into integrated neighborhoods (Seitles, p. 3). Another form of overt racism was showed in an analysis of data from the Home Mortgage Disclosure Act which showed that African Americans and Hispanics applying for home mortgage loans were more likely than whites to be denied credit and showed discrimination based on minority status. The study showed that minorities experience discrimination 50% of the time and also pay a "discrimination tax" of $3,000 every time they search for a house to buy (Seitles, p. 6).These practices become a major obstacle for minorities and force them into neighborhoods that are affordable but low maintenance, are high in crime, have limited community services, and have inferior schools. Minorities that are surrounded by high crime rates become affected by this because they are prone to get involved with the wrong people in the neighborhood and commit crime as well. Forcing African Americans and other minorities to live in areas with limited community services reflects in their behaviors because the community lacks the resources to combat crime and find a common ground of values. Unlike whites, these neighborhoods don't have the money to create programs to keep minorities out of trouble or assist them in financial or community problems which in turn creates higher rates of crime.

Seeing that the critical race theory believes racism is used in laws to maintain White supremacy one can conclude that zoning laws are in fact a form of this argument. In the way that governments can zone out unwanted property, they do in fact maintain white suburban supremacy. Although affordable housing is meant to assist poor minorities it is also an asset for whites as well. In the way affordable housing is not integrated in white suburban neighborhoods this "protects all white neighborhoods" that way minorities are unable to move into suburban areas. Zoning practices as well as the "discrimination tax" for minorities looking to buy houses keeps blacks and Hispanics from buying houses in white neighborhoods. Section Eight and the use of steering minority individuals into deteriorated, low income homes, and in communities primarily of minority background are common practices that in fact maintain white power and black oppression. Minorities are subdued in the sense that they are forced to live in neighborhoods that are prone to crime and hardships. White power is saved because blacks cannot come into neighborhoods and force whites to move and decrease property value. These practices are unfair and prove that racism is a norm in American society in the way that minorities are not offered the same opportunities as whites or a chance at upward mobility. Critical race theorists would agree that crime fluctuates in poor neighborhoods because minorities are forced to live in crime infested areas and receive a lack of resources and inferior schooling due to white supremacy and interest convergence.

Evidence from "Critical Perspectives on Race and Schooling" supports racial disparities in the critical race theory. In 1995, Gloria Ladson-Billings and William F. Tate established critical race theory to the education research community and connected it with its understanding for racial disparities in education achievement, funding, curriculum, suspension, expulsion, graduation rate, and education assignment inequities (Ladson-Billings, 2012). From then on CRT became an analytic tool to understand education inequalities dealing with race. Critical Race scholars in education focus on the way race determines education and schooling outcomes. Again, even in education "interest convergence" persist throughout the topic. In fact, CRT scholars have argued that even when polices are put in place to benefit minorities, the policies ultimately benefit whites. An example of this focuses on school funding disparities between urban and suburban districts. Jonathan Kozol, a social commentator, described a $10,000 disparity between these districts and found that minority students experience less valuable assets than Whites. In other words, Black students take fewer academic courses, fewer honor level courses, and fewer Advanced Placement courses (Ladson-Billings, 2012). A special case noted that a minority student was denied admission to a college after receiving a 4.0 because she didn't take AP classes. However, she did not have the opportunity to take AP courses because they weren't offered at her segregated school.

Many studies also show disparities in discipline, minority students are suspended at higher rates than white students for less serious actions. Statistics of low income black students show that they are suspended and expelled at higher rates than whites (Ladson-Billings, 2012). A study of the improvement of New Orleans schools have brought concerns to the University of Minnesota's Institute on Race and Poverty who suggest that this experiment does not serve all students well. The study found that the state reorganization of schools created a separate but unequal structure system of schools. This structure segregates white students into high performing schools and steers majority of low income students to high-poverty and low performing schools (Ladson-Billings, 2012).

Property value is a major concern to critical race theorists. It proves that the importance of property is essential when understanding racial and ethnic inequality in the sense that minorities receive less valuable property than whites. For instance, the former assets mentioned earlier as well as the fact that poor communities have a limited amount of resources and are unable to support schools and assets. After using these findings as evidence to CRT, scholars in fact believe that race is a permanent feature of society and it has an impact on both equality and quality of schooling as well as crime. Education in CRT is important to connect race and crime because the fact that race influences minorities' chances at the quality of school also influences their chances in upward mobility and staying out of crime. If minorities are receiving less assets, inferior curriculum, more suspensions, and lack of positive guidance and good teachers, one can conclude that they have a better chance at exceeding in crime than in school.

Lastly, evidence from "Divergent Social Worlds" by Ruth Peterson and Lauren Krivo can be used as evidence to back up the critical race theory. In this article there is a close connection between race and crime across individuals in the United States. Statistics show that although minorities are disproportionately populated compared to whites, they make up for majority of criminal offenders in the United States. For instance, in 2007 African Americans represented 39 percent of people arrested for violent crime and 30 percent of those arrested for property offenses yet they only make up 13 percent of the population (Peterson & Krivo, 2010). Statistics like this prove that nonwhite individuals or minorities are overrepresented as crime offenders. This data also proves that crime is disproportionately concentrated in cities or communities where more African Americans reside (Peterson & Krivo, 2010). It is clear that the criminal justice system targets minorities and African Americans more often than whites and proves that whites benefit from living in neighborhoods underpopulated by minorities because there is less crime. The act of racial profiling and stop and frisk explains why minorities are so overly represented because they are targeted for their race. This supports CRT because these laws that allow overt discrimination and prejudice explains the relationship between race and crime. This is a form of victimization because minorities are victimized into being criminals just because of who they are.

An important study connects this evidence on race and crime. Mary Pattillo-McCoy focused on the heightened risk of crime and violence in a middle-class black community in Chicago due to its location near troubled African American areas. This study found that race-based patterns of segregation create problem areas and residential options (Peterson & Krivo, 2010). However, a contrasting study done by Patrick Carr found that residents of white working class neighborhoods in Chicago fended off crime, violence, and gangs through participating in organizations that create alliances with institutions, for example, the city council, the police, and even education that can provide resources and practices to prevent crime and maintain social order. Zoning practices as well as recreation programs also serve as methods to create social control and reduce crime. The study found that nonwhite neighborhoods lacked experience with these types of forms of social control and access to resources (Peterson & Krivo, 2010). Again one might conclude that segregation is that sole factor for crime in minority neighborhoods. Whites segregating themselves from black neighborhoods and creating methods to fend off criminals benefits white neighborhoods but in the end affects minority neighborhoods. These minority neighborhoods are unable to create social control because minorities do not have the ability to create alliances with the police, city council, or schools which leads to crime.

Overall, the Critical Race Theory believes that laws and policy makers protect White supremacy and power through the way race is normalized and instilled in practices and policies which benefit Whites, the continuation of minority oppression, and the experience of minorities to further analyze and prove how discrimination still takes place on a daily basis and causes crime. In "Residential Segregation" CRT is proved through which policies protect white suburban areas and segregate minorities into ghettos and illegitimate crime prone neighborhoods. In "Perspectives in Education" CRT is essential when providing statistics on racial disparities and minorities' lack of property value assets which lead them down a path of crime instead of education. In "Divergent Social Worlds" the disproportion of minorities in the criminal justice system points to racism which is designed to keep African Americans incarcerated. It further proves that the lack of resources and opportunities digs minorities into a deeper hole of crime and inequalities. In every aspect the Critical Race Theory provides evidence which proves that race is an important factor of crime.

By: Bianca Perry, Class of 2015

REFERENCES

Aguirre, A. (2000). Academic storytelling: A critical race Theory of affirmative action. Sociological Perspectives, 43, 319-339.

Bobo, L.D, & Charles, C.Z. (2009). Race in the American mind: From the Moynihan Report to the Obama candidacy. Annals of the American Academy of Political and Social Science, 621, 243-259.

Buckelew, R., & Burton, L. (2010). Critical race theories, colorism, and the decades research on families of color. Journal of Marriage and Family, 72, 440-459.

Gabbidon, S.L., & Greene, H.L. (2005). Race and crime. Thousand Oaks: Sage Publications.

Hylton, K. (2010). 'Race' and sport: critical race theory. Contemporary Sociology, 39, 224.

Ladson-Billings, G. (2012). Critical perspectives on race and schooling (perspectives in education). Encyclopedia of Diversity in Education. Banks, J. (Ed.). Thousand Oaks: CAS Sage Publishers.

Peterson, R., & Krivo, L. (2010). Divergent social worlds: Neighborhood crime and the racial spatial divide. New York: Russell Sage Foundation.

Seitles, M. (1996). The perpetuation of residential racial segregation in America: Historical

discrimination, modern forms of exclusion, and inclusionary remedies. Journal of Land Use & Environmental Law: 1-8

Taylor, Edward (1998). A primer on critical race theory. The Journal of Blacks in Higher Education, 19, 122-124.

THE CRISIS OF INCARCERATION

Incarceration is a rather large issue in society today, and certainly one that should not be overlooked. In recent times, there has been a strong upheaval due to issues of police brutality that has taken place in places such as Ferguson. Many people have different versions of what occurred the night that 18-year old Michael Brown was killed by a Caucasian male police officer. It is my opinion that the differences in reactions by the public stem from their understanding of race. After that evening, there was a strong light that emanated and put into the spotlight the harsh treatment of African Americans in that town in addition to the distrust between city officials and the citizens in that town. As the events of that evening were under investigation, the story became rather twisted and tainted due to several rumors, media coverage, etc. There were some witnesses that brought forward the fact that Brown surrendered by putting his hands up right before he was shot and killed. There were others that said he put his hands up, but continued to move towards the police officer. However, overall it seems that there were different reactions to the shootings between those of white racial background in comparison to those of African American race.

According to the article that was written on People Press, "Blacks are about twice as likely as whites to say that the shooting of Michael Brown 'raises important issues about race that need to be discussed'" (People Press). To me, this is a rather interesting statement due to the following reasons. It is quite evident that there are some very important issues about race that need to be discussed. They need to be discussed in our classrooms; they need to be discussed in our homes, offices, etc. There is so much ignorance that is present in the world due to the misinformed minds of our youth and those who influence them. Racism is very much alive in today's world although powerful, strong, leaders such as Dr. MLK took a stand in order to end racism. However, my main question is why is it that white people do not see the issue of racism as clearly as African Americans? In the article a statistic raises an important point by stating, "By about four-to-one (80% to 18%), African Americans say the shooting in Ferguson raises important issues about race that merit discussion. By contrast, whites, by 47% to 37%, say the issue of race is getting more attention than it deserves" (People Press). This statistic is so important. Why do people of color see race as an issue that needs to be discussed? Could it be because of the many years of oppression that African Americans went through under the hands of white supremacy? Isn't it a fact that there are some white people still alive today that consider themselves to be superior to African Americans? The oppression that African Americans went through caused them to want to seek justice and equal opportunities as the white man. This is what the Civil Rights Movement stood for. However, it seems that today, history is repeating itself once more.

Another way to view this issue is politically. As we look at the differences between each political party, we see that there is a stark difference in views. The article states, "Republicans also are more likely than Democrats to view the police response to the Ferguson shooting as appropriate and to express confidence in the investigations into the incident. More Republicans think the police response has been about right (43%) than say it has gone too far (20%). Democrats by 56% to 21% say the police response has gone too far" (People Press). I have always wondered why it is that Republicans do not like to discuss issues of race as being rather important. I believe one main reason for the stark differences in the political viewpoints of republicans is due to the white privilege. Many people who grow up around the Republican Party do not experience many of the hardships those of the other party experience. Many of them are rich, white males and females that are not taught to value race. According to the statistics, it is quite evident that race is a major issue that needs to discussed in order to educate the population and bring to light many of the issues that African Americans undergo in everyday society, that white people may not think about. So how do we do this?

Educating our children to the realities of this world is very important. Of course doing this at an appropriate age is also something a parent should take into consideration. Our children need to learn and know of the harsh realities and issues of race that people face every day. Discussing these issues may not make our children advocates and leaders, but it will open their eyes and allow them to be much more mindful of the issue of race and how it affects society. Parents and teachers must learn to educate our children about race and teach them to be open-minded to learning about the cultures that are alive in other parts of the world. Those who grow up in privileged families do not always see the harsh realities that others in the world go through each day. For instance, if we were to analyze the events and thoughts that led up to what occurred the night that Brown was killed, we should ask ourselves why is it that Michael Brown had to steal? There are many factors that one needs to look at when answering this question. They revolve around education, socioeconomic issues, race, etc. In my opinion, race and political affiliation should not be ignored when it comes to examining the guilt or innocence of Darren Wilson. Clearly, Mr. Wilson should have had more of an empathetic approach to dealing with this situation. Do they teach empathy in the police academy? However, let us just presume for a moment that he did take an empathetic approach and did not kill Michael Brown. What if the situation was flipped so that it was Michael Brown who killed a police officer? What would be the outcome then? The current outcome of this case is that the US Department of Justice cleared Wilson of the civil rights violations in the shooting. It found that the witnesses who corroborated the officer's account were credible, but the ones who incriminated him were not credible. Let us think for a moment who would corroborate his story, and who would incriminate him. Those who take issues of race seriously could see that without a doubt, this is an issue of race! If the situation were flipped and Brown shot the officer, he would be facing a sentence of life in prison. Evidently, there is an issue of race in this country that is not being discussed. Although incarceration is a crisis in our country, it is a response to an even larger crisis of our justice system being ruled by white supremacist leaders who do not take into consideration issues of race in their everyday work.

By: Mohamed Abdallah, Class of 2016

UNTITLED

I try to refrain from watching the news because the constant violence is heartbreaking and the way it is broadcasted makes it sound satirical. Grant you, the ignorance is sometimes comical but recently I have not even almost cracked a smile at news headlines. A society where it is legal for a white male to blatantly murder a black male, with evidence, camera footage, witnesses, for no reason at all and walk free of charge and sentencing is not amusing to me. Murder is heinous and deserves the ultimate punishment. At the point in time when you decide you are going to take someone's life, you are inheriting all Godly abilities, boldly accepting that you have the power invested in you to do so.

We live in a society where racism and prejudice is still very much alive and we're told to "let it go" and "move on." If it is not hurting you personally then you don't understand how it is hurting other people. If you do not see this as a problem, then you are instantly part of the problem. We live in a society where we have had an African American president, yet it seems as though we have regressed in history; it seems as if we have taken steps back into a time of segregation. We have taken so many steps back that I do not feel as if we progressed at all; we are the new slaves in blinded society. We are distracted by so many things that are asinine that we do not understand. Baltimore is not only in state of emergency but America, the United States of America, a country allegedly built on unity and diversity is in a state of emergency, code red, and has been for many years. We as a people must do better.

Black lives have a purpose in this world and it seems that purpose is not visible to our white opponents and in order to rectify the "problem," (yes black people are said to be a problem) they must kill us off. This is no different than the mass murder of Jews in the Holocaust, this is a genocide of black males, they are trying to reduce our existence in society.

We have sat back and watched countless young black men lives be snatched away from them before their time. We watched senseless premature murders happen repeatedly. Now it is our time to react.

Malcolm X said over 50 years ago that we are not a people who are anti-white, we are a people who are anti-oppression and our consistent oppressors just happen to be the white male. We didn't ask for this to happen, we are not sure why it is happening, but the problem does not seem to be going away. X says that time isn't running out, that time has ran out. That we are no longer willing to be level headed about this, we are no longer compromising our lives, our born rights, or our freedom, and we are no longer willing to take a Martin Luther King stance on this. This calls for a little more radical approach. No, burning down our cities is not the problem solver here but you have to understand that we are a people who are broken, we have come to our end. Our brothers, our sons, our fathers, and our loved ones have been taken away from us, we do not know why, but we are in mourning. So forgive us for no longer knowing how to react rationally to such disregard of black lives; if we do not matter then that same blind eye that is shut over our importance should remain shut over the disruption happening in the city of Baltimore. Vancouver was turned upside down by rioters when Canucks lost the final in the Stanley Cup. Stores were looted, cars were set on fire, and police officers were taunted and that was over a hockey game... a hockey game. But people can not seem to understand why Baltimore residents are unhappy that Freddie Gray's life was lost due to police brutality and died in their custody, America is at a loss as why people are reacting the way they are. We are fed up, we want justice, we want our sons to leave our homes and return safely. The talks we give our young men have changed; when a cop stops you, simply obey and listen to everything they say even if you know you have done nothing wrong, do not by any means run, or reach for a phone. Simply just listen to what they are telling you, so you can make it back to your families.

How many more lives have to be taken before America realizes that they are doing something wrong, before they see that this is a problem, before they realize that we bleed just as red as they do and that our lives, black lives, do matter. These people are rioting on behalf of the crimes our law enforcement system has caused; if a few destroyed cops cars and trashed buildings mean more to you than the life of Freddie Gray then the issue has just increased severity. Police have been detaining these crowds and rioters without gun violence, does that mean we can stop a young black male for questioning without it resulting in his murder? Black lives matter and I will not sit silently and watch America devour its babies.

By: Jule Keese, Class of 2018

IN HEAVENLY PEACE

Do you dream of heaven
To get away from Earth?
Because you feel so trodden down
And no one knows your worth?
Life is simply color,
Blurry hues of dark and light.
And no one harks or stops to see
Your heart of gold shine bright.
Do you pray to get to heaven,
Where all the angels see?
That you were so much more
Than just a numbered casualty.
And when you get that Heavenly peace
For so your heart did yearn,
You weep that life has gone away,
On Earth hate still does turn.

By: Maisha Mayazi, Class of 2015

QUESTIONS

Unit 1: Wake Up, We Have a Problem

1. What personal challenges are described by the authors of this unit? Have you experienced or witnessed similar instances of racism and/or racial injustice in your own life?

2. How do the readings in Unit 1 challenge the notion that the United States is a country of equality and unity?

3. Pick any two readings from Unit 1. Compare and contrast how race in the United States of America is depicted throughout the two pieces.

4. Re: I Am Going to Tell You My Story (Choices)

    In "I Am Going to Tell You My Story," the author speaks of a black boy who is caught "between a web of choiceless choices and the pipeline to prison." What do you think Kromah means by "choiceless choices"? In what ways does our society limit the options of young African Americans?

5. Re: "Wake Up! Wake Up!" (Progress since MLK)

    Over fifty years ago, in 1963, writer James Baldwin said:

    "What white people have to do is try to find out in their hearts why it was necessary for them to have a nigger in the first place. Because I am not a nigger. I'm a man. If I'm not the nigger here, and if you invented him, you the white people invented him, then you have to find out why. And the future of the country depends on that. Whether or not it is able to ask that question."

    If Baldwin were alive today, do you think that he would conclude that we've made progress since 1963 (the same year that MLK delivered his "I Have a Dream" speech)? Has our society been able to ask that fundamental question? Why or why not?

6. Re: Critical Theory on Race and Crime (Colorblindness)

    Some argue that, as a society, we should be moving toward the goal of colorblindness (e.g., not allowing racial identity to be a factor in decisions regarding social policy). Others argue that colorblindness perpetuates racism, because it doesn't acknowledge existing white privilege and its consequences for people of color. Is colorblindness something that we should strive for or something we should guard against? Why?

7. Re: The Increasing Income Gap (mass incarceration and forms of racial control)

   In her book The New Jim Crow, Michelle Alexander argues that mass incarceration, via the "War on Drugs," functions in much the same way that Jim Crow laws did -- as a form of racial control that keeps African Americans voiceless and powerless within our society. What are other ways in which federal/state/local laws and policies function to segregate our society and disempower African Americans?

8. Untitled (Black Lives Matter)

   The Black Lives Matter movement originated in response to the 2013 acquittal of George Zimmerman, after being charged with the 2012 killing of Trayvon Martin. The movement grew in 2014, after the deaths of Michael Brown (Ferguson) and Eric Gardner (NY). The "All Lives Matter" slogan was created in response to the Black Lives Matter movement, which some perceived as suggesting that non-black lives don't matter. Imagine that you are responsible for mediating a conflict between two individuals, one who argues that black lives matter and the other who argues that all lives matter. How would you approach this? What assumptions does each side make? Do you think this argument can be resolved? If so, how? If not, why not?

UNIT TWO

Race In America: Is It Learned?
Could It Be About Fear And Power?

The readings in Unit 2 grapple with questions about the origins of racism and racial violence in America. Together, these texts ask, "How can this happen, and what can we do about it?" Through a mix of personal and scholarly writings, this section puts forward theories of racism's causes and effects, in the words of students studying and experiencing these phenomena in a variety of situations. As students bring their own knowledge and experience to bear on these questions, they offer important perspectives about race. Both inside and outside the classroom, these selections can help readers reflect upon their own understanding of how racism develops and circulates in our culture.

MR. BROWN

Click Clack! Sweat was sliding down my face

Bang! I was reflecting about the actions taken that wiped me without a trace.

Now, I am looking down from these white cloud skies

At all the chaos of the unarmed men crying goodbyes.

Filled with unanswered questions I wonder about Mr. King

He said, we are fighting this war to commence the declassifying.

For the color of my skin that holds years of judgment

Unfair accusations, suffering pain and injustice is constant.

Just a silver badge with a title and some clothes

Elevated to human rights abuse that followed.

Many of us make mistakes through life, we learn and grow

Did it have to be taken to full measures when I received that blow?

I refuse to complain of what took place

Lives are ending because of brutality with no whiteface.

Boom, Boom, Aghh! Are the sounds we hear of a dead man down

So are you doing the job or taking advantage through the whole town?

The problem started with racism and has dispersed as violence

While innocent unarmed civilians are protesting in silence!

With all the noise what's in the ruins lies confusion and miseries

Authorities have elevated to the road crossing all the boundaries.

Do not stand behind, rise for our rights and values

Gather the evidence so solutions make way to these issues.

Equality, justice and peace have fallen upside-down

But everywhere hope and love calls for the people to speak for Mr. Brown.

By: Joshua Fields, Class of 2017

THREE READING RESPONSES ON RACE

Learning how to be a racist

I grew up in many places: Collingswood, Camden, & Monroeville, NJ; Philadelphia and Scranton, PA; Quito, Ecuador ... and now Natal, Brazil. As a child, most of my time was spent in the first three locales. As a child, I never really thought about race, but I knew people in Monroeville definitely looked at and spoke about persons of color a lot differently than Camden. Take a ride down 55 and you will see what I am talking about. Cowtown, its rodeo, or the music festivals that come into the Salem County Fairgrounds have parking lots with Confederate flags waving proudly.

We are only 150 years removed from the abolition of slavery. Which means it is feasible that my grandmother (who died at 90 a couple years ago) met someone who either owned a slave or had an opinion on it. This probably affected her opinions on people of color.

There is a poignant scene in the movie 42 where a father and a son of a highly impressionable age are watching a baseball game. Jackie Robinson comes out and the father goes on a slur-filled tirade, while the son looks at him, absorbs what is going on, and then mimics him, booing "that nigger." I imagine a lot of people learned to hate like this young boy.

Redscape/Greenscape

I never really watched someone die before I watched the Eric Garner footage. I mean, of course I see people die in the news from grainy security footage, but I never saw someone struggle like Garner. I wept for quite some time during and after the video and had a moment of crisis: if I care so much about this, why am I not dedicating my life to it like Colin?

My friend Colin quit a job he loved in education and went to law school. He incurred tens of thousands of dollars of debt, studied hundreds of hours, and became a public defender in Milwaukee, Wisconsin whose metro area is the most segregated in the country. I admire Colin because he actively is a voice for the voiceless and vulnerable. He is working to become more proximate to our most vulnerable populations through the judicial system. Colin sees a problem and tries to eradicate it by removing it ("redscape")

I am not willing to do what Colin did to fix this problem, but that doesn't make me less committed to fixing it. I practice a "greenscape" approach: promoting good instead of eliminating the bad. I worked the past four years in admissions at Camden Catholic High School (full disclosure: my alma mater). Recently, students painted a mural in the school which includes words or pictures symbolizing their experience at Camden Catholic high school. Three words the students chose stand out to me: diversity, acceptance, and empowerment. The high school is probably the most socioeconomically diverse in the region and the biggest daily discipline problem is uniform code and gum chewing. Students from inner city Camden study alongside

students from the ritzy suburb of Moorestown and they more than accept each other ... they love one another. Because of this learning and loving experience, they become empowered young men and women. I firmly believe that every student I convinced to come to Camden Catholic which exposed them to such diversity was greenscaping racism.

The Right Thing

Both redscape and greenscape are important to a solution, but alone, one can't redscape every problem in the world, whether that is racism, hunger, or poverty to name just a few. We cannot dedicate ourselves professionally to so many things, but we can greenscape them in our daily lives. One simple way is through discussions: overt and wrought with all the difficulties that come with it, or subtle conversation with familiar people or strangers. Another way is suggesting excellent movies to people who may be still reading like Spike Lee's Do The Right Thing. Here is an irresponsible quick synopsis which will not give the movie justice:

On the hottest day of the year in Brooklyn's Bedford-Stuyvesant section, the movie focuses on an Italian-run pizza shop founded by Sal whose main patrons are black. Racial tensions spill over into the night, which leads to the demise of Sal's pizza place.

The movie ends with the following Dr. Martin Luther King quote:

> Violence as a way of achieving racial justice is both impractical and immoral. It is impractical because it is a descending spiral ending in destruction for all. The old law of an eye for an eye leaves everybody blind. It is immoral because it seeks to humiliate the opponent rather than win his understanding; it seeks to annihilate rather than to convert. Violence is immoral because it thrives on hatred rather than love. It destroys a community and makes brotherhood impossible. It leaves society in monologue rather than dialogue. Violence ends by defeating itself. It creates bitterness in the survivors and brutality in the destroyers.

That is proceeded by:

> I think there are plenty of good people in America, but there are also plenty of bad people in America and the bad ones are the ones who seem to have all the power and be in these positions to block things that you and I need. Because this is the situation, you and I have to preserve the right to do what is necessary to bring an end to that situation, and it doesn't mean that I advocate violence, but at the same time I am not against using violence in

self-defense. I don't even call it violence when it's self-defense, I call it intelligence. – Malcolm X

The movie is a tremendous work of art. It left me uncomfortable the first time I saw it. Truthfully, it leaves me uncomfortable, and I have probably watched it a half dozen times.

Juxtaposing those two quotes after two hours of witnessing subtle and overt racism always leaves me confused. I don't endorse violence, but with every Ferguson or Baltimore riot, we are presented with an opportunity to have a national discussion, a line that Barack Obama has tip-toed with soft quips, but never crossed with hard conversation. I believe too that the riots give us an opportunity to do more greenscaping or at the very least remind us we can greenscape.

Too many people didn't care about Baltimore or Ferguson until peaceful protest turned for the worst. It is because of the rioting some are just becoming aware of racism and yet some simply don't understand or care. I also believe that despite whatever we may have heard, the most important resource in the world isn't money or oil ... it is humans. Not just white humans, nor black, brown, yellow, tan, dumb, smart, "good" or "bad." All humans. And we are doing an awful job proving this to the rest of the world. I hate thinking this, but if racism is going to be solved organically (and completely peacefully), it is going to take time. Lots of time. More time than my grandmother potentially knowing a slave owner. It will take longer than my nonexistent children's or grandchildren's life time. And it shouldn't take that long.

By: Marc Vallone MBA Student, Class of 2014

IN AMERICA

In America, we are quick to divide ourselves, to hate each other, and to jump to violence. We so often forget that we are stronger when we unite, we are better when we love each other, and that it truly feels better to forgive than to hold a grudge.

We can say that racism doesn't exist anymore because of some laws that passed and movements in history, but those thoughts only serve to feed our guilty conscience.

It's true, segregation is not a law anymore, but we have chosen to keep it in place. We segregate each other, through wealth, stereotypes, and racism.

These divisions are what we, as a society, created. Toni Morrison recently said in an interview, "There is no such thing as race. Race is a construct; a social construct." We created the concept of race and racism. All humans have 99.9999% the same DNA. There is only one race and that is the human race.

Martin Luther King frequently called us all brothers and sisters and he made no distinctions, when he said that. He was right to do so.

However, I realize that it may be difficult to view society differently, so I'd like to share with you all my light in this darkness.

In high school, I made three best friends: Quinones, Rachel, and Shavonte. Quinones is Black and Indian. She is a Muslim who lives in a single parent household in one of the poorest areas of Baltimore. Rachel is Chinese and white. She is an atheist who lives with her mom and dad in one of the wealthiest parts of Baltimore. Shavonte is black. She is a Christian who lives with neither her father nor her mother. She lives nowhere because she is homeless.

We all live different and imperfect lives. But we still love each other.

We try each other's foods. We make jokes and laugh together. We take silly pictures and dress up in ridiculous outfits together. We tell each other secrets and keep our promises. We love each other so we've never abandoned each other.

When one of us was in trouble and had to go to detention, we all sat in detention with her. When one of was bullied, we stood up for her. When one of us was down, we held out our hands. When one of us was in pain, we were all in pain. We would go to the ends of the earth for one another and that is true love.

In Martin Luther King's time, no one could fathom that people of different races, religions, and socioeconomic statuses could love each other so deeply. But Dr. King saw it, when no one else did. He was killed for his dream, but he died fighting for a better world.

From civil rights leaders to women activists, we are a people that refuse to conform and keep quiet. Fighting for justice is required of a nation that preaches freedom.

However, the greatest enemy of change is not cowardliness, but ignorance. If I said justice was upheld in America, I'd be a liar. Injustice is still prevalent in our society.

In America, the media sexualizes women, thereby making it seem as if we only have one purpose.

In America, rape victims are condemned more than rapists.

In America, people are dehumanized based on who they fall in love with.

In America, hate is spit at others for whom they pray to at night.

In America, some students can't go to college, not because their grades weren't high enough, but because they couldn't afford it.

In America, the schools in the ghetto are the worst schools in the nation because they lack the proper resources to educate and motivate their students.

In America, an officer can walk out of court free, after murdering a young black teen with no weapons or felonies, while a black teen can shoot a dog and go to jail for twenty three years.

In America, not all little girls can feel like princesses. I should never hear a five year old girl tell me that she wants soft hair and white skin so that she can be beautiful, too.

I'm aware these discussions may be uncomfortable or painful to hear about. But could you even begin to imagine how much more agonizing it would be for the victims who must struggle with the world and their identities every second of the day?

As human beings, we must open our eyes to injustice, open our ears to the voices that tend to go unheard, and most importantly, we must open our hearts to love.

By: Nadine Benavides, Class of 2018

TRIBALISM DEPICTED IN TWILIGHT: LOS ANGELES 1992

One of the most impactful events in history showing the effects of racial discrimination was the Rodney King riots in Los Angeles in 1992. These riots became so escalated that Anna Deavere Smith, an actress, went and interviewed many different people about these events. From these interviews she took excerpts and created the play Twilight Los Angles: 1992. Through the format of this play Smith is able to clearly depict a theme of tribalism. Within this theme the audience is able to see how people of a "tribe" show feelings of close mindedness and resentment, and how this causes tension among different groups. However, in the end she implies how problems of inequality could possibly be solved, and how peace could be found if one steps away from their tribe by looking through a different pair of eyes.

Before one dives into some of the significant speeches it is important to note how one should refer to Tribalism in the context of the play. In a production note on the play Smith mentions that "This play is about race relations and the degree to which we make assumptions about others based on the first visual impression they make" (5). This is important because it implies that Smith is using this play to get across a message about how people group themselves together based on race and how people are judged immediately because of their race. In the play people also become defensive of their own racial group. However, this idea can be expressed in judging people of different social classes and professions as well. So, when a tribe is referred to we are not talking about an actual native tribe but a group of people who are similar in some way, like race or financial status.

One feeling of tribalism that is expressed in this play is the need to protect others of their own race. One prominent example of this is the "My Enemy" speech spoken by Rudy Salas Sr. He talks about how "at school first grade, they started telling me I was inferior because I was Mexican." (29) Right away from this statement the audience is quickly able to identify what the conflict is. Rudy is described as an older man in his sixties so it is clear that from a long time ago, some feel that there is a social hierarchy among people of different races. Rudy goes on to say that, "I realized I had an enemy ... those nice-white-teachers" (30). The fact that he chooses the word enemy is very interesting because usually when there is an enemy there also has to be a good guy fighting for justice. This implies that Rudy is very defensive of the Mexican race. When Smith portrayed him on stage he was seen to be stomping around and getting progressively louder with each sentence. This makes him appear very aggressive which implies he's not afraid to show feelings of anger or hatred towards others of different tribes. It also shows what Smith mentioned earlier about first impressions. Rudy did not like some white teachers therefore he dislikes all white people.

Why else is it though that Rudy feels wronged by the white people? He explains that when he was in his teens he was physically beaten up by white cops (30). He was so scarred by that event that he became fearful and "had a hate" (30). He says, "If I would read about a cop down the street ... I thought maybe he's one of those motherfuckers y'know" (31). Due to the harsh events that happened to him, he now assumes that all white cops hurt people. He must go against their entire tribe. He even says at the end, "I don't even see them as whites" (32). This means that he is unable to see them as a tribe. All he can see them as is an enemy. All of this speech shows how due to unnecessary harshness it has caused Rudy to be on guard and alert about "whites" or other non-Mexicans hurting him or people of his own tribe. It's interesting that Smith gives the point of view of a Mexican because on the surface the Rodney King issue seems like something of black vs. white. However, with showing the views of a Mexican it seems she is trying to show us that there are problems between all races due to the tribalistic views.

While Rudy expresses the feelings presented in the rioters, Smith also presents people who grouped themselves together without being directly involved in the riots themselves. This view is expressed in the speech of Elaine Young, a white real estate agent. She tells the story of how she and a date had to go to the Beverly Hills hotel during the riots. In her speech some words are exaggerated such as, "Everything is closed" (78) and "I mean it was mobbed" (78); when the play is performed Smith chooses to really project and annunciate these words. It's almost like Elaine is trying to overdramatize the events of the riots to make it seem like she is sympathizing with everyone. But, really if you look at the event itself she just stayed with the "picture-business-people" (78) or her own tribe. She says the hotel was "like a fortress" (79). In reality this event can be seen as very close minded, she watched the riots from a distance and only cared about her own safety with people of like mindedness. She did not actually interact with the "tribes" involved in the riots.

Even though the first two attitudes depicted in the play were very negative ways of looking at it, there were some characters who showed optimism and hope. Cornel West, a scholar interviewed in the play, describes optimism as "based on the notion that there's enough evidence out there to allow us to think things are going to be better." He describes hope on the other hand as when one "looks at the evidence and says this doesn't look good at all." West continues to say that people with hope "make a leap of faith beyond the evidence ... to create new possibilities" (106). Based on this definition the clearest example of a character with hope turned to optimism is Twilight Bey, an organizer of a gang truce. He explains, "When I talked about the truce back in 1988 that was something they considered before its time" (170). It can be interpreted from this quote that people thought Twilight was ahead of his time because the gangs were in such bad shape during 1988. No one ever thought they would make peace. Since Twilight was looking at a positive idea during a time of despair, he could be considered hopeful. He goes on say, "But in 1992 we made it realistic" (170). It is important that note that realistic is written on its own line. This emphasizes the point Smith is trying to make that people can ignite change if we step away and make peace. Twilight can now be considered optimistic because he has real facts to back up his faith. He made his vision a reality.

Gangs are very similar to tribes and it is clear that Smith and Twilight are making the point that if we look past our judgements of who belongs to what group we can find peace. This is further explained by Twilight by saying, even though he feels like he's in a world of darkness, "I see the light as knowledge and the wisdom of the world and understanding others" (171). Twilight is using the comparison of light and dark to the events going on to explain that we can move forward into the light or more positive things by gaining knowledge and learning about the thoughts and feelings of others rather than just how us or our group feels. A person has to step out of their tribe. This idea is continually prominent throughout the play with not only characters like Twilight but, also characters like Mrs. Young Soon Han. She was a Korean woman included at the end of the play who even though still bitter was able to admit that she was able to sympathize with the black people (people not of her own tribe) and feel happy for them even though she felt Koreans still needed justice. Smith is giving the idea that people have to take a walk in others' shoes to gain better understanding and peace.

Overall, Twilight Los Angeles: 1992 gives us a very real and honest depiction of what was going on during the time of the riots. Not only does Smith give us the bitter angry side of one tribe in the beginning but also, the closed off uninformed side of another. However, the most important thing that she gives us is the message of opening ourselves up to others and not grouping ourselves into one single tribe. The play shows us that by looking at events through different perspectives we can gain more knowledge and move forward towards a world of peace. This is a strong impactful message that is able to remain in the reader's hearts forever.

By: Jordan Harlon, Class of 2018

A RESPONSE TO "SUPERIORITY" BY ADAM PHILLIPS

In Adam Phillip's discussion of equality and superiority, he uses Chantal Mouffe's Democratic Paradox to help characterize democracy as agonistic pluralism. Mouffe says that a place of democracy is one in which equals engage in conflict. Phillips adds that "the equality in Mouffe's version of democracy, such as it is, could never be an equality of wealth, or talent, or beauty. The only equality that exists in it is in each person an equality of riveness, an equality of unknowingness, the equality born of there being no foundations to master" (13).

I thought this description of the equality of man as a universal inability to completely understand or completely manipulate the systems under which he resides was quite interesting because it renders society a construct not of specific mastery, but rather, "temporary forms of consensus" (13). Temporary forms of consensus which are key in a democratic society address the fluid "pluralism of values" as Mouffe described, and allows equals to engage in discourse and conflict in the form or talking, listening and disagreeing–all things similar to the experience of psychoanalysis according to Phillips, fuel an "appetite for democracy" (12).

Phillips says that a goal of analysis is to make the patient at least receptive towards the views of others. Through the process of analysis, the patient would stop trying to suppress conflict in the form of an authoritarian order such as the super-ego, and would actually seek it through various social engagements as he says that speaking itself "is worth doing because it is conducive to conflict" (13). I think that the therapeutic value can be seen here because it strays the patient away from thinking that one perspective is supreme and encourages him or her to challenge and consider many perspectives that are considered to be equal.

Adam Phillips goes on to say that "conflict that is not between equals ceases to be conflict very quickly. It becomes the simulacrum of conflict called sado-masochism" (12). My understanding of sado-masochism is that it is the pleasure derived from the infliction of pain. It is about dominance, authority and control. It is the same driving force that perpetuates a worldwide culture of rape and exploitation.

Phillip's discussion of sado-masochism as being the conflict of those who are not on equal playing fields, reminds me of a conversation I had recently with my roommates Jill and Joanna. In an article Joanna and I had read for Dr. Volpe's class regarding the banking crisis of 2008, Mark Dempsey says that "blaming the borrowers for the problem loans is like blaming a rape victim for dressing too provocatively."

This sparked a lengthy and heated discussion about how the entire poor and middle classes are victimized and demeaned (or essentially raped) by the wealthy investor class. Just as the sadistic nature of rapists thrive off of the fear and vulnerability of their victims, the greedy nature of the upper class is satisfied by the insecurity of the lower classes flailing for stability. It is an issue of power. Just as the rape victim lives her life constantly looking over her shoulder for imminent danger, the poor and middle class citizen participating in modern American economics similarly lives under the constant fear that they will lose everything—the ultimate form of submission. But there doesn't seem to be a choice for the victims of oppression as they seem to be no match for the oppressor.

I think that Adam Phillip's initial discussion of the human desire for superiority is quite important in this context. He argues that this desire stems from the need for people to "exclude themselves from something" and their "need to reject something in advance. They must in one way or another, be untouchable" (7) to achieve dominance. The invincibility of being untouchable only works when the victimizer can be sure of the outcome, however, because his superiority was somehow "guaranteed in advance" (7). The sheer size and physical power of a man can give him the means to strip another individual of consent just as the sheer size and political power of big business and the state-finance nexus, allows the super-wealthy to strip this country of equality. In both cases, the victimizers' superiority was guaranteed in advance. If the simulacrum of conflict; which is intended to be an equal exchange, is sado-masochism, than the simulacrum of democracy is present day America. Are we in need of some psychoanalysis?

By: Yasmin Attia, Class of 2016

REFERENCES

Phillips, Adam. "Superiorities" *Equals*. Basic Books, 2002.

IT'S BEYOND THAT

First, I would like to begin by discussing the definition of law. The definition of law as listed in our Business Law textbook on page three is, "Law, in its generic sense, is a body of rules of action or conduct prescribed by controlling authority, and having binding legal force. That which must be obeyed and followed by citizens subject to sanctions or legal consequences is a law." I would like to focus on the phrase "prescribed by controlling authority… and followed by citizens," it seems as if sometimes we forget that police officers are citizens as well. We are all human, we all make mistakes and most importantly we all have emotions that can cause us to make poor decisions. Therefore I personally believe that the recruitment process of police officers needs to be more strict. If we make the recruitment process more strict we might have to also increase the salary of police officers as well, but in the end we will have better police officers and also a more fair and honest judicial system.

Next, I would like to discuss the Equal Protection Clause that was added to the U.S. Constitution in 1868. On page seventy-six of our Business Law textbook under Equal Protection it reads, "The clause prohibits state, local, and federal government from enacting laws that classify and treat "similarly stated" persons differently … Note this clause is designed to prohibit invidious discrimination." Our 14th Amendment protects against discrimination yet there are officers of the law wrongly and fully discriminating everyday? Could the protests going on across our nation, resulted from police killing citizens, have been avoided if discrimination wasn't so popular among police in certain areas? Well we will never know for sure, but I can say discrimination happens everywhere. It's not just white cops discriminating black citizens or black cops discriminating white citizens, it's beyond that. Here's my personal story.

I live in a very diverse area, five blocks from Camden, NJ and about six blocks from Collingswood, NJ. Camden is predominately colored people, while Collingswood is predominately white and the town I live in, Woodlynne, is a mix, but mostly black and Hispanic. When I was younger the police force in my town was majority white and my friends would always tell me to talk to the police any time we were out pass curfew or riding our bikes without helmets on. I knew they wanted me to talk because I was white, but I always told them they were crazy, the cops aren't going to bother them because they're colored. The only cop that ever bothered us was a white cop, but he also bothered me too. We were young and he was mean, but never actually did anything to us.

Then, my junior year of high school I watched a cop beat up a colored kid on my front lawn, but I just assumed he did something to deserve it. Then sometime between my sophomore and junior year of college my town hired an entirely new police force. So when I returned home for winter break I no longer knew any of the officers; the force was predominately black and Hispanic. The first five days I was home for break I was illegally stopped and frisked by police three times. I was harassed about twice after that by police. Once was even on my own property. If this isn't discrimination at its finest I don't know what is, especially after not finding anything illegal in my possession the first three times I was stopped. The officers assumed I was just some white kid walking through Woodlynne to get to and from Camden, which is a high trafficked drug area. Unfortunately, they were incorrect and I am just a resident of a predominately black town. With better police, incidents like this can be avoided and the Equal Protection Clause can be enforced.

By: Ervin Ray, Class of 2015

RACISM AND VIOLENCE

Violence is seen as the way out

Abandoned children, hunger and war

Lead to inhumanity and chaos

Discrimination and racism are taught

At a tender age

And that's what we now surround the children in

It is not the color of the skin

But the impact on society that matters most

Peace, love and unity

Are what matter most

Across the entire globe

By: Tasfia Aminur, Class of 2018

QUESTIONS

Unit 2: Race And America: Is It Learned? Could It Be About Fear and Power?

1. According to the readings in Unit 2, where do our ideas about race come from in the United States of America?

2. Using any three readings from this unit, discuss why race is a challenging concept to define.

3. In your own experience, how have your definitions of race and/or racism changed or developed over time?

4. Pick one reading for which you would like to be able to respond directly to the author. What would you say, and why?

5. What is the difference between "redscape" and "greenscape," according to Vallone in Three Reading Responses on Race? How do we know when each is called for in a particular situation? Which do you feel more called to and why?

6. In "Tribalism Depicted in Twilight: Los Angeles 1992" the author explores the connection between tribalism and racism. Do you think that human beings are, by nature, tribal? Do we need to overcome tribal identification in order to become a more just society? Why or why not?

UNIT THREE

Being "Black"

Unit 3 offers student perspectives on what being "black" means in the United States. Current and former La Salle students explore black identity and black experiences in America. La Salle student writings in this unit express what blackness is and how it becomes constructed in the United States, from their perspectives. In particular, this unit focuses on the issues of negotiating black identity and the problems inherent to navigating the challenges presented to black bodies in the United States. In all, this chapter offers reflections about the nature of black experience and the violence enacted against black bodies in America. These readings can help readers to build empathy toward greater understanding of the troubled and terrifying black experience in America today.

COLOR ME BLACK

Color me black

Brown to be specific

Like Mike Brown

Another Man down, man down on the floor

And Once more There's one more

Skeleton added to the cold closet

Of injustice...

It's just this System of corruption

That gets these spirits up in flames

Burning to the core

With those battle scars and sores

That our brothers and sisters first handedly witnessed

As victims

And they won't let us forget to remember

A past so devastatingly dismembered

That's still trying to be put back together

By the blood...

The bloodshed from just talking

The blood loss from only walking

The bloodbath they gave for marching

So you can call me Martin

Like Trayvon or Dr. King

Same thing because of the color of their skin

That meant something

But at the same time meant nothing

They were black.

And when they died that's what we were to dress in

And so we go on mourning

Morning, noon, night

It just seems like

No matter what time of day it may be

They still manage to find the darkness

In our eyes

In our lives

In our skin

And fail to realize that we are not JUST our pigmentation

We are more

We are a nation And Red, black and blue are the colors of our flag of freedom

Because that's how we were colored after being beaten

And killed

And shunned

And hung

And maimed

So color me black... 'Cause I'll never be ashamed

By: Tamar Noisette, Class of 2017

#BLACK LIVES MATTER

Waking up every day BLACK is a struggle, to say the least, and no one can fully comprehend the magnitude of what it means to be BLACK unless they in fact are black. In America there is no other race that is so hated, mocked, ridiculed, or unjustly treated as that of black Americans. A race of people unwillingly captured, sold, and forced into a cruel and oppressive way of life with no hope of returning to their homeland and somehow generations later we have managed to gain a crumb from that forever humbling "American Pie," often times forgoing the rights entitled to us by the Constitution, voluntarily or involuntarily, just to survive. I say that to say this, the topic of justice has long been a sensitive subject for the black community. Black people have never felt equality when it comes to justice whether on the defense or prosecuting side, and more than just a feeling of inequality, history has proven that black Americans do not have equal access to justice.

The Los Angeles riots were a "social explosion" (251), as Gladis Sibrian put it in Twilight, a buildup of racial tensions and people tired of feeling violated. Rodney King was the spark and Latasha Harlins, the 15-year-old schoolgirl murdered by the Korean grocery store owner, the detonator. The sentence that Soon Ja Du, the murderer of Latasha Harlins, received can hardly be viewed as punishment. Ms. Du was convicted of voluntary manslaughter, a crime that held a maximum penalty of 16 years in prison, yet Judge Karlin, a white female judge, only sentenced Du to five years' probation and a $500 fine. Justice was not served because the punishment given was not equivalent to the crime committed. Flash back 30 years before Latasha Harlins to Emmett Till, a 14-year-old black boy murdered in 1955 for speaking to a white woman, and then fast forward 21 years after Latasha to Trayvon Martin, a 17-year-old black teen murdered by a nosy citizen after shopping in a 7-11. The murderers of both Emmett Till and Trayvon Martin were found not guilty. So history and the present mirror themselves prove that if you feel threatened by someone black, it is open season and more likely than not a juror of "your peers" will justify the actions you take. So how does that make the black community feel? Well, being black, I'll tell you: it makes me angry, I feel enraged, I want to fight, kick, and curse because no one seems to care, not even those we charge with upholding the law, how it feels to lose your loved one for something so miniscule as $1.89. Judge Karlin obviously felt sympathy for Ms. Du, but where was her empathy for Latasha Harlins' mother? If Judge Harlin could relate to Latasha Harlins' mother even a finite amount I am certain that the sentence delivered to Soon Ja Du would have gone differently.

I must admit that at the start of reading this book I didn't understand why Korean merchants were being targeted in the riots but after watching the movie Twilight and learning of Latasha Harlins' death it became evident. Empathy, whether we would like to admit it or not, plays a major role in justice; it is easy to point a finger and stand on the proverbial soap box to complain about the injustice "our" people are experiencing but what about our fellow man? Do we ever put our selfishness aside and stop to think about our fellow man and their loss experienced? Because in all these experiences not everyone is a winner: "they finally found justice ... they got their rights by destroying innocent Korean merchants ... that destroy innocent people and I wonder is that really justice!" The words of Ms. Young Soon Han make anyone with half a heart wonder where is the justice for the Korean merchant who did not kill an unarmed black school girl but are guilty of nothing more than having the name Yoon, Park, Han or So and owning a store in the wrong neighborhood. But in the same interview Ms. Han puts aside her hurt: "In a way I was happy for them ... at least then they got something back ... and I have a lot of sympathy and understanding for them. Because of their effort and sacrificing." While Ms. Han obviously feels the Korean population was not served justice, her humanity allows her the ability to recognize that justice was not served for another community as well.

Anna Deavere Smith, after sitting through the Rodney King civil trial in Simi Valley, said " ... perceive how profoundly different our experiences of law enforcement can be" (xix). As a reader, that statement means to me that justice is like beauty and it is in the eye of the beholder. As people we all view things differently based on our experiences and those experiences are what influence our judgement when delivering justice because other than that we have nothing to go on. We are making an attempt to deliver justice on information we have received second hand and Harland W. Braun alludes to just that in his interview in Twilight: "Even Clinton who I like ... says 'Justice has finally been done.' how does he know? And I know, I think I know what happened out there...I mean, I think" (241). All we have are the words of either party and all we can do is pick a side and stand on it and hope that its right because ultimately no one really knows but the two parties involved, the truth. So to me that means that justice can never truly be served, that someone will always be the sacrificial lamb, and Harland Braun agrees: "is it better that two innocent men get convicted that fifty innocent people die?" Who has the answer to that? All one can do is seek empathy so that we can feel the other person's pain and learn from past mistakes.

In conclusion, the question is not really of justice being served but the "shades of loss" (xxi) felt once justice has been "served." For me Twilight made me question humanity. What happened to love for thy fellow man and being thy brother's keeper? Rodney King was beaten senseless and violence committed against him only begat more violence, more hurt, more pain, more loss, and more victims. If history has proven one thing, while aching for our lost brothers, such as Freddie Gray and Michael Brown, further community violence will not get our point across efficiently. Justice will come no faster because we are only feeding the stereotype of being ignorant, angry, and animalistic. Justice will be served when each one of us learns empathy for another. I am someone's daughter, sister, wife, mother, and friend and by seeing that in others and not skin color, educational background or economic status we can start to break down those barriers that prevent true justice from being served. At the end of the day we must remember we are all a part of one race and that is the HUMAN race. #ALL lives MATTER

By: Shameka Bowser, Class of 2017

THEN WE SHALL SEE FACE TO FACE:
Absalom Jones and His Theology

The history of Black America is filled with fiery and inspirational religious leaders. From Nat Turner to Malcolm X and Martin Luther King to Cornel West and many others, religion has been an integral part for many blacks towards equal rights and liberation from white supremacy. Considering the seeming importance of that religious element to African American history in the United States, I turn now to an individual that I see as an oft overlooked part of that legacy, Absalom Jones. His story, in many ways, is one of black defiance and perseverance in an unjust society stacked against African Americans in nearly every way. His life is also a story of incredible service and selflessness. Throughout this essay, I hope to show the connection between the events Absalom Jones faced in his life and the theology that he would come to develop.

Additionally, I believe that the story of Absalom Jones is massively important not only to African American History, but to the history of Philadelphia. During his lifetime, Jones was of massive service to the city of Philadelphia as a whole. This service will be discussed in depth when we look at Absalom Jones during the Yellow Fever Epidemic of the 1790s. Besides his service, Jones was an extremely influential man during a time which came to shape the character of Philadelphia. The role that Jones played in the larger historical narrative of Philadelphia cannot be overlooked.

A Life From Servitude to Service

Absalom was born into the institution of Slavery on November 6, 1746 in Sussex County, Delaware.[1] He was owned by Benjamin Wynkoop, a budding merchant in Philadelphia who sold various groceries such as coffee, chocolate and rum. Wynkoop would later be a vestryman and church warden of Christ Church and St. Peter's Church. In his childhood, Jones worked on the plantation that Wynkoop's parents owned. It was during this time that Absalom's mother and his six siblings were separated from him and sold off. Following that, during his adolescence, Absalom worked in Benjamin Wynkoop's grocery store.[2]

Over the course of these crucial teenage/early adult years Absalom was able to work towards his freedom. Wynkoop allowed him to work night shifts and keep his earnings. Additionally, Absalom spent some time learning

---

[1] St. Thomas Historical Society. "About Absalom Jones, Founder." African Episcopal Church of St. Thomas.
[2] Safford, Tim. "Who Owned Absalom Jones?" Christ Church.

mathematics and literacy at a local school owned by Quakers.[3] Fatefully, he was also able to acquire a copy of the New Testament during his education.[4] Apparently this education was received with the blessing of Wynkoop.[5] Nevertheless, Absalom wasn't able to buy his freedom until 1784, after he had spent 38 years in slavery. As soon as he was free, Absalom and his friend, Richard Allen became preachers at St. George's Methodist Church. A Church whose white leadership welcomed whites and blacks.[6] Around this time, Absalom adopted the last name of "Jones." [7]

Throughout his life, Absalom Jones was often mistreated or ignored by members of the white religious community. Tim Safford, Current Rector of Christ Church, asks why Wynkoop's church took no moral responsibility for Jones throughout his period of enslavement. He asks, "Why did his Church, who had many abolitionists as members, remain silent?"[8] The implication is that the reason was because Wynkoop was a fairly high ranked member of Christ Church's community. Additionally, while at St. George's, Absalom Jones did a fair bit of evangelization in the surrounding community. That evangelization multiplied the membership of the church by 10, however this brought them little recognition or respect from the leadership of that church.[9]

In fact, over time, while Jones was at St. George's, racial tensions mounted. Eventually this led Absalom Jones, Richard Allen and their followers to leave the Church.[10] One key incident in the early 1790s that led to drastic action of the part of Jones occurred at the start of a Sunday service. Black members were suddenly expected to sit on balconies that had been constructed in the back of the church. Absalom Jones asked that he would be able to remain in his usual seat for the duration of the opening prayer. However, two ushers decided that Jones had to be relocated immediately; they lifted him and dragged him over to the back of the church. The black parishioners (including Absalom Jones and Richard Allen) marched out of the church en masse following the prayer.[11] This occurrence represents a tremendous act of self-assertion on behalf of the African American community in Philadelphia. It is

---

[3] St. Thomas Historical Society
[4] "Celebrating Absalom Jones." New York Amsterdam News.
[5] Safford
[6] New York Amsterdam News
[7] St. Thomas Historical Society
[8] Safford
[9] St. Thomas Historical Society
[10] Ibid
[11] Raboteau, Albert J. Canaan Land: A Religious History of African Americans. Oxford: Oxford University Press, 2001. 23.

an incident is a significant one that we will revisit in the theological section of this essay.

Following this event, Absalom Jones was involved in the founding of a couple of predominantly black churches in Philadelphia, notably AME Bethel and St. Thomas. Jones was nominated as pastor of St. Thomas' in 1794, at age of 48.[12] St. Thomas was the first black Episcopal church in the United States, this was the church he would eventually be buried at. It was also, in many ways, an outgrowth of the Free African Society (a society that Jones had helped bring forth). Later in his life, Absalom Jones was also elected First Grand Master of the African Masonic Lodge of Pennsylvania.[13] In the heart of Philadelphia, Absalom Jones had helped build the black religious establishment. We will revisit this fact when we look at James Cone's view of Absalom Jones and Richard Allen.

When the yellow fever hit in 1793, Absalom Jones and the Free African Society aided the multitudes of sick people piling up in the city. Members of the Free African Society functioned as nurses, tending to those infected with yellow fever. Jones and five other black men (whom he hired) at one point hauled bodies left piled in houses and streets to local graveyards. At times, Jones filled in for his friend Benjamin Rush (a prominent physician in Philadelphia) and administered aid to the sick.[14] Benjamin Rush wrongly believed that blacks were immune to the disease. Nevertheless, Jones and other blacks worked tirelessly in aid of sick Philadelphians black and white.[15] Later, Absalom Jones and Richard Allen published an account of the "yellow fever" to capture the horrors of the disease. This publication also served as a documentation of the contributions of blacks during the epidemic.[16] It was, in part, a response to claims that the blacks intentionally mistreated whites during the epidemic. The book would make Jones and Allen the first published black authors in America.[17]

Years after the Yellow Fever epidemic, Absalom Jones was ordained as a priest into the Episcopal church at Christ Church. (the church that both Benjamin Rush and Jones' owner belonged to).[18] Interestingly, Absalom was married at Christ Church on January 4, 1770. On that day he was married by

---

[12] Ibid

[13] St. Thomas Historical Society

[14] Powell, J. H. Bring out Your Dead; the Great Plague of Yellow Fever in Philadelphia in 1793. Philadelphia: Univ. of Pennsylvania Press, 1949. 95-102.

[15] Benjamin Rush's Home and African Methodists' Role in the Yellow Fever Epidemic." Philadelphia Methodist History Walking Tour.

[16] Powell

[17] "St. Thomas African Episcopal Church." Methodist History Walking Tour.

[18] Philawalk St. Thomas

Reverend Jacob Duche to Mary (who was a slave to the King family).[19] At the time both Absalom and Mary were slaves, the fact that they were both owned by different families and they were allowed to marry strikes me as odd. Nevertheless, it seems as though Absalom Jones had a relationship with the predominantly white Christ Church his whole life.

The Theology of Absalom Jones

At this point, I would like to consider a few different ideas about theology (specifically black theology) and look at how Absalom Jones' theology fits into those ideas. Doing this, we will be able to get a sense of Jones' place in black theology overall. In this section we will examine primary sources towards that end. One document is a transcript of a sermon he gave on Thanksgiving 1808. The other, An Address to Those Who Keep Slaves and Uphold the Practice was written in 1794. Together, I hope to glean the value of those ideas to the history of black theology.

Here, I'm going to explain the different perspectives I'm keeping in mind while looking at the writings of Absalom Jones. The first is the idea that theology acts as a sort of reference point and vocabulary for describing the world in which we live. This view may appear dry and overly sociological but on the contrary it enriches the theology and uncovers unseen layers of meaning. Many authors have explained this view in the past but I think Ludwig Wittgenstein (an Austrian Philosopher of language) explained it best as "Theology as grammar."[20] The basic idea is that religious and spiritual belief (along with other kinds of ideological beliefs) provide structural guidelines for describing the world around you, words that you might not have otherwise.

Another concept I'm going to be keeping in mind is the idea of black theology as being "prophetic." Cornel West, an African American philosopher and theologian, described what propheticness means in an interview with the New York Times. He says "Black prophetic fire is the hypersensitivity to the suffering of others that generates a righteous indignation that results in the willingness to live and die for freedom."[21] What I take him to mean is that propheticness in black religion is a mindset that uplifts and pays attention to the voices of those who are disadvantaged and suffering. In that way black theology is prophetic in that it emulates what West would say is the approach of the prophets in the Bible.

Now, I turn to the theology of Absalom Jones. Following are excerpts from a sermon Absalom Jones gave on Thanksgiving 1808 at St. Thomas' African Episcopal Church. Here is a telling excerpt from that Sermon. He says: Our

---

[19] Christ Church Archives, Carol Smith
[20] Wittgenstein, Ludwig, and G. E. M. Anscombe. Philosophical Investigations. 116.
[21] Cornel West: The Fire of a New Generation." New York Times. August 19, 2015.

God has seen masters and mistresses, educated in fashionable life, sometimes take the instruments of torture into their own hands, and, deaf to the cries and shrieks of their agonizing slaves, exceed even their overseers in cruelty. Inhuman wretches! though You have been deaf to their cries and shrieks, they have been heard in Heaven. The ears of Jehovah have been constantly open to them: He has heard the prayers that have ascended from the hearts of his people; and he has, as in the case of his ancient and chosen people the Jews, come down to deliver our suffering country-men from the hands of their oppressors. He came down into the United States, when they declared, in the constitution which they framed in 1788, that the trade in our African fellow-men, should cease in the year 1808: He came down into the British Parliament, when they passed a law to put an end to the same iniquitous trade in May, 1807.[22]

Clearly, Absalom Jones is describing God as a deliverer of the oppressed. Additionally, Jones claims that the "cries and shrieks" of the downtrodden are "heard in Heaven." Here, I think, we can see a version of what Cornel West describes as Prophetic. Its propheticness stems from the way it centers suffering at the heart of its concern. For Absalom Jones, there is a history of God being amongst the suffering of others, especially slaves. He details the different instances in which he thinks God came down to be in solidarity with slaves.

Absalom Jones really brings all of this home when he says, "The history of the world shows us, that the deliverance of the children of Israel from their bondage, is not the only instance, in which it has pleased God to appear in behalf of oppressed and distressed nations, as the deliverer of the innocent, and of those who call upon his name."[23] This, even more than the other quote, shows the prophetic concern and prioritization of the oppressed in Absalom Jones' theology. The presence of this propheticness is important from an intellectual perspective because it's a feature of American black theology that is found throughout history and even up to today. Historically, it's important because, chronologically, Absalom Jones was among the first (in the then-brand-new in 1808) African American religious establishment to articulate this concern towards the oppressed.

Using these quotes we can also understand Jones' theology as a means to spell out the conditions in which he lives. For example, he relates to the Constitution ending the slave trade and the British parliament ending the slave trade through religious expressions. Jones characterizes these events as occurrences as events where God "came down" to deliver those who were suffering from their oppressors. In this way, we can see that Jones relates

---

[22] Jones, Absalom. "A Thanksgiving Sermon." Antislavery Literature Project.
[23] Ibid

these events as events with divine significance. Looking more deeply, we can see a subdermal framework in which Absalom lives. His perspective reveals this sort of periodic and unending cycle of moments in which the abused are truly affirmed. I think that this cyclical view of Christian theology is somewhat unique and lacks a certain finality that is sometimes implied in Christian worldviews. Moreover, the idea that God "comes down" is a very kinesthetic kind of imagery that implies that God is not something that is above us, but rather among us.

Another key primary document that we can use to understand the theology of Absalom Jones is a writing of his entitled An Address to Those Who Keep Slaves and Uphold the Practice. As mentioned before, it was written in 1794, fourteen years before his Thanksgiving Sermon. Within, Jones writes: "We do not wish to make you angry, but excite your attention to consider, how hateful slavery is in the sight of that God who hath destroyed kings and princes for their oppression of the poor slaves; pharaoh and his princes with the posterity of King Saul were destroyed by the protector and avenger of slaves."[24] Notwithstanding the fourteen year difference and the different intended audience (this text was intended for a white audience), the message remains surprisingly consistent between this writing and his 1808. For Absalom Jones, it is clear that God stands (as Cornel West would put it) prophetically with the downtrodden and the enslaved.

This writing is also evocative of a point made by James Cone, an African American Theologian and an important thinker in the Black Power movement. He writes in regards to Nathan Paul, a 19th century black minister, "Nathaniel Paul can only affirm his faith in God in view of his assurance that God hates slavery and that his righteousness prevails over evil."[25] Cone says, for the slave, God had to hate slavery. This characterization of God hating slavery fits very well with the approach Absalom Jones takes. Jones himself says that God sees slavery as "hateful."

Indeed, I think that the story of Absalom Jones fits many of James Cones' ideas about Black Power and the theological role of humanity in black religious thought. An inkling of these ideas can be found in an interview Cone did with Bill Moyers on the PBS show The Journal. Cone says: "I know God is present when I see little people ... the least of these ... affirming their humanity in situations where they have few resources to do that."[26] When Jones, Allen, and the blacks of St. George's' left, were they affirming their

---

[24] Newman, Richard S. Pamphlets of Protest: An Anthology of Early African-American Protest Literature, 1790-1860. New York: Routledge, 2001. 41.
[25] Cone, James H. Black Theology and Black Power. New York: Seabury Press, 1969. 96-98.
[26] Moyer, Bill. "Interview with James Cone." PBS.

humanity? When Jones and Allen helped create a black religious establishment in Philadelphia, were they affirming their humanity? When Jones and Allen became the first published African American authors, were they affirming their humanity? I think so. And above all, affirming it in the face of unimaginable economic and cultural obstacles. Here, I think we can see Cone's insight into the character of black American theology.

However, I must disagree with Cone's characterization of Absalom Jones in one regard. In his book, Black Theology and Black Power he writes, "The very existence of the black church meant that men like Richard Allen and Absalom Jones were convinced that the evil of racism in the white church was beyond redemption."[27] I do not agree that Absalom Jones believed the evil of racism in white churches was "beyond redemption." In fact, it seems to me that he spent a great deal fighting for the redemption of the white religion. It's true that he helped create a safe environment for African American religious community in Philadelphia that further separated the black religious community from the white religious community; however his writings and actions make me believe that Jones hoped that this separation would ultimately be temporary. This is reflected in the relationship that Jones maintained with Christ Church, a predominantly white church, throughout his life. It's also reflected in his writings, for example, addressing a white audience with Richard Allen, the pamphlet An Address to Those Who Keep Slaves and Uphold the Practice reads "We wish you to consider, that God himself was the first pleader of the cause of slaves."[28] It seems as though Jones wished to cause a change in the attitude of the white religious community towards the personhood of slaves. He urges them to recognize that God gave slaves humanity too.

In conclusion, I think it is plain to see that Absalom Jones played a massive role in the religious history of Philadelphia at the very least. Additionally, it's also apparent that Absalom Jones certainly deserves a place in black theology. What can we learn from Absalom Jones? I think in Absalom Jones we learn that great leaders and thinkers can emerge even from communities that are disadvantaged. Further, I think we can also learn that those who are downtrodden can find a truth in a dominant belief system that might be obvious to those who "own" that dominant belief. In any case, the story of Absalom Jones is a valuable one.

By: Alex Palma, Class of 2016

---

[27] Cone 137
[28] Newman 41

REFERENCES

Benjamin Rush's Home and African Methodists' Role in the Yellow Fever Epidemic." Philadelphia Methodist History Walking Tour. http://philawalk.org/rush/

St. Thomas African Episcopal Church." Methodist History Walking Tour.http://philawalk.org/index/#/thomas/

St. Thomas Historical Society. "About Absalom Jones, Founder." African Episcopal Church of St. Thomas. http://www.aecst.org/ajones.htm

Raboteau, Albert J. Canaan Land: A Religious History of African Americans. Oxford: Oxford University Press, 2001. 23.

Wittgenstein, Ludwig, and G. E. M. Anscombe. Philosophical Investigations. 116.

Safford, Tim. "Who Owned Absalom Jones?" Christ Church.http://www.christchurchphila.org/Welcome-to-the-Christ-Church-Website/Who-We-Are/Sermons

Christ Church Archives, Carol Smith

Celebrating Absalom Jones." New York Amsterdam News.

Cornel West: The Fire of a New Generation." New York Times. August 19, 2015. http://opinionator.blogs.nytimes.com/2015/08/19/cornel-west-the-fire-of-a-new-generation/

Jones, Absalom. "A Thanksgiving Sermon." Antislavery Literature Project. http://antislavery.eserver.org/religious/absalomjones/religious/absalomjones/absalomjones.html.

Newman, Richard S. Pamphlets of Protest: An Anthology of Early African-American Protest Literature, 1790-1860. New York: Routledge, 2001. 41.

Moyer, Bill. "Interview with James Cone." PBS.. http://www.pbs.org/moyers/journal/11232007/watch.html.

Cone, James H. Black Theology and Black Power. New York: Seabury Press, 1969. 96-98. Powell, J. H. Bring out Your Dead; the Great Plague of Yellow Fever in Philadelphia in 1793.

STRUCTURE FROM DAD

Structure is important in the household.... What's the first thing you see when you look at me?

Is it the head full of flowing locks? Is it the eyes that could make Madonna melt or the devilishly dapper attire which coordinates from head to toe?

Well before all of that, it's structure. That unique imperative for a man: structure. Shoulders up, chest out, back straight: structure. That can't be taught in too many ways and if you can't get it in the household, the streets will teach you.

See, single mama can teach you, but so many things: how to walk, how to talk, how to ride a bike, how to read and write, how to be polite, how to treat a woman right and even how to fight, but not how to be a man. She could never fully translate to you that structure: always needed pops for that. Without it, these children are left with no choice, but to search for that structure in the streets. My generation worships these false idols like they were their ancient ancestors and they would murder to be mirror images of them. There are so many children left forsaken in this nation that could turn into honors scholars with the teachings of a father, but no one knows.

The so-called guidance counselors are left puzzled in the school systems trying to figure what these children are missing when the men of today have the answers in their mere presence. The cure is readily available. These kids don't need out of school suspension, they need paternal attention; parental extensions. They don't need diagnostics as much as to admire fathers. These children don't need Ritalin as much as some compassion, don't institutionalize our youth give them structure.

The importance of a father is downplayed in today's society only because there are so few that play the role right if at all. Hip Hop culture has made it cooler to have a baby-mother than a wife; cooler to have a seed than a son; cooler to dodge child support than to raise a household. Being a father is not portrayed as necessarily cool and that is not necessarily cool.

It's not cool when I walk into a classroom of 25 4th-grade inner city students and I ask by show of hands how many of you know the lyrics to this new 2 Chainz song and get 25 hands, and when I ask how many of you look up to your dad I get 10.

I have a dream which is deeply rooted in the American dream. I have a dream that one day all of my little cousins will have someone to look up to other than the hottest rapper on the radio. I have a dream that one day all of my brothers will step up to the plate and decide to raise what they have made. I have a dream that one day there will be one father figure to every single child in America. And my dream goes on.

I grew up with my father my entire life and he's always been there beside me, teaching me structure. It wasn't until I turned about 15 that I realized I was the only one of my friends that had that and it made me start to question.

Never should my friends have to feel envious of me for having a loving pop nigh should I have to feel embarrassed around them for the same reason. This trend has to end somewhere, soon. My pop never had a dad like him. He made a promise to himself at 13 that he'd be better than his father ever was. I made myself a promise to myself at 19 that I'd be an even better father than mine.

The question I pose to all of my men out there is what kind of father will you be?

Make up your mind quick 'cause these little brown boys and girls are in need of some structure.

The urgency is now.

By: Erick Bey, Class of 2014

UNTITLED

    I want to start by saying I love where I come from and who I have become. I am proud to be who I am, and wouldn't change any of it, but there is always room for improvement, and there is always room for recognition, realization, and reflection. Being African American on top of being a female comes with its fair share of challenges, but I am honored to be who I am. With that being said, we, my people are always fighting for equality, fairness, and looking to be treated like everyone else, but when we do hold ourselves to the same standard? Yes, I am all for equality and truly believe that we are not defined by the color of our skin, but it is only in us, my people, that I find we create more division amongst ourselves than do the people around us. We are always looking to blame the next person for our problems and hardships, but what are we doing to help ourselves? Light skinned, caramel, brown skinned, and dark skinned. My people are the only people I know who have created a race within a race. We see each other through different lenses because of the color of our skin, but expect everyone else to see us equal. My people, we teach others how to treat us by the way we treat ourselves. We have created division amongst each other and have decided that this one and that one aren't good enough. There are all sorts of stereotypes associated with the complexion of someone's skin, and they come from us, our very own people. We cannot continue to ask society to treat us a certain kind of way when we do not even treat ourselves with the same kind of respect. I love us, my people, and I am proud to be a part of such a dynamic race, but we have to stop placing the blame and pointing the finger. We, my people, have to hold ourselves and each other accountable, and then we can work on changing the perception the world has, but in order to change the world we must start with ourselves. So, I said all that to say this: we, my people, must begin to treat ourselves according to the standard we hold everyone else to, and with that, we will begin to see change for the better.

By: Ebony Wells, Class of 2015

SKIN

The color of my skin

does not define me.

I am not

Belligerent

Rebellious

Odious

Worthless or

Nefarious

I am just a person

Who shouldn't be labeled by the dark stains

that inhabit my almost, perfect skin.

I am just a person

who will not allow the syringe of weakness and defeat to be

injected into my body

I am immune to the eyes that dart to the left

as I walk to the right

Immune to those poisonous words that

causes others,

fear.

By: Shantal Perez, Class of 2020

ILLUSTRATION: THE OPPRESSOR'S VISION

By: Jasmond White, BA 2019

QUESTIONS
Unit 3: Being Black

1. What are some of the challenges of being black in the United States of America, according to the authors of Unit 3?

2. How do these pieces help us understand how history and context affect the life experiences of African Americans today?

3. As you read, make a list of similarities and differences of what being black means to the authors of Unit 3.

4. How have the readings in Unit 3 influenced your own ideas about what "being black" means in the United States of America today?

5. In #BLACKlivesMATTER, Bowser suggests that empathy plays a major role in justice, while at the same time observing that no one can fully understand what it means to be black without being black. Is it possible to experience empathy without a full understanding of another's experience? What, if anything, enables us to do this? How might we as a society work to cultivate empathy when our lived experiences might be very different from one another's?

UNIT FOUR

Prejudice and Discrimination:
Beyond Black and White

In the United States, discussions of racism often focus primarily if not exclusively on tensions between white and black people and communities. In Unit 4, La Salle students refocus those conversations to engage with issues of prejudice and racism beyond blackness and whiteness. In personal reflections, artwork, and scholarly analysis, students wrestle with the challenges faced by Hispanic/Latino, Native American, and Asian communities. In exploring from undocumented immigrants to Islamophobia, microaggressions and glass ceilings, these students challenge prevailing conversations about racism and push the discourse beyond black and white. In addition to shining light on other marginalized groups, such as those with disabilities, the texts in this unit may prompt reflection on intersectionality and racism between and among communities of color.

ILLUSTRATION: JIM CROW LIVES

By Conor Coleman, BA 2016

HISPANICS

My parents obtain their news from Univision, the Spanish broadcast network with the most properly spoken Spanish around[29]. Chapter 5 of the Halbert and Ingulli book took me back to the days before living in Pennsylvania, days where the TV in the house was on with regularity at a volume I would've preferred have been lower. Lozano v. city of Hazleton was a case of the first kind in the US, aimed at making life for illegal immigrants so difficult they would rather leave[30]. This held our family's attention, the community in San Antonio and many communities across the nation as it was all the Univision could air. This chapter has moved me to look into the case, it has begun to help me think through stereotypes, immigrant integration, through Illegal Immigration Relief Act (IIRA), and to face the contradictions I feel when almost anything surrounding immigration is discussed.

The IIRA proposed by Hazelton's mayor in July 2006 penalized employers for hiring illegal immigrants and landlords for renting to them. It was claimed they were a threat to public safety and affected quality of life by imposing stresses on the city caused by the unauthorized entry of many. The lawsuit challenged the IIRA on the grounds that federal immigration law preempted the town's right to pass its own laws[31].

Hispanics as the largest growing minority in the United States is a fact understood by many, but not accepted by the same. Much like Hazleton, the impact is especially different in places not used to the diversity of immigrant communities. Integration in these smaller towns makes it challenging as visibility is higher; migrants going undetected is virtually impossible[32]. The sudden entry of legal and undocumented Hispanics to the town of Hazleton arose from the terrorist attacks in New York as people sought better opportunities. Because of enacting IIRA, Hazleton has been unsuccessful in accepting newcomers. In the very least, the integration of Hispanics living there legally could be more accepted instead of lumping and making the assumption that all Latinos are undocumented.

The latest ruling for Lozano v. Hazleton came earlier this year, stating "...the U.S. Court of Appeals for the Third Circuit in July 2013 rejected

---

[29] Univision strips their on-air personalities of any, well, personality, of any accent. Unnecessary information, I understand, but I felt the need to share.
[30] http://www.nytimes.com/2013/04/01/us/politics/lessons-for-republicans-in-hazleton-pa.html?pagewanted=all&r=0
[31] Halbert, Terry. Law & Ethics in the Business Environment. PG 130-133
[32] . Zuniga and Hernandez-Leon. New Destinos: Mexican immigration in the United States.

Hazleton, Pennsylvania's anti-immigrant housing and employment ordinances, confirming that the laws, which have been continuously blocked under earlier federal court rulings, are unconstitutional and should never go into effect. The ruling came in a lawsuit filed by the ACLU of Pennsylvania...[33]."

Though these IIRA ordinances are not enacted in Hazleton today, there have been impacts to this town, business owners, landlords, local officials, native residents, Latino residents, and other cities, too. My ever-contradicting feelings of understanding the need to punish criminal activity are at odds with recognizing the undocumented immigrants were my parents, at one point, who just wanted the opportunity to work hard and make a fair living. Simply, this could be the beginning contribution of my ethical voice. While Hazleton today can in some small capacity recognize the revitalization brought on my immigrants, some are finding it insensitive how city officials and city natives continue to contrast illegal immigrants against "...older waves of European newcomers..."[34]. According to the ACLU, Hazleton officials continue to argue that the town's "...ills, including crime and economic burdens..." are to be blamed on the undocumented immigrants—all without evidence, that is. I can't help but see this issue as an opportunity for Hazleton to learn about and model integration.

By Hermilla Duran, MBA 2014

---

[33] https://www.aclu.org/immigrants-rights/anti-immigrant-ordinances-hazleton-pa

[34] http://www.nytimes.com/2013/04/01us/politics/lessons-for-republicans-in-hazleton-pa.html?pagewanted=all&r=O

UNTITLED

My left hand massaged the right as our group discussion on immigration came up. My classmate stated her opposition to illegal immigrants except for when she leans on this group of people for cheap labor. She went to clarify that her distaste was for uneducated illegal immigrants—as if this corrected her previous statement. I couldn't help but notice a slight spoken accent and couldn't keep from becoming tense. Without losing eye contact with sincere curiosity, I asked her to explain. As she continued, I tried to understand her experiences and was challenged. The conversation forced me to begin putting words to my personal challenge with any immigration conversation, noting the difference in terms "illegal immigrant" v. "undocumented immigrant," as immigration conversations sparked throughout the week.

My conversations regarding immigration and surrounding issues are relatively new vocabulary for me. Up until my move to Philadelphia, I've lived in major Hispanic communities and some very inclusive neighborhoods across the United States and really didn't have the need to defend a stance. You see, my parents were once these undocumented immigrants that some are so scared of. They braved a walk across the desert for days with only hope in their eyes and courage in their pockets. Today, they are citizens of this country, proud, without a formal education, but in many ways, more educated than many folks that proudly hang recognition on their walls. I know numerous undocumented immigrants across this country and am ashamed of none for they are willing workers wanting a chance to prove themselves.

Maybe I'm too close to the issue, too close to see what native people of this land or the difficulty those people too far removed from their own immigrant story have in seeing how not very different the current wave of immigration is from older waves of immigration that built this country. The irony that America is often referred to as the "country of immigrants," but as time passes, appears to be accepted less and less isn't lost on me. The difference I see is that the undocumented migrants today are too many years too late.

Interestingly, in my continued research both online and in conversation with friends, I noticed a difference in terminology: illegal v. undocumented immigrant. As I read up on the use of language, articles confirmed the term chosen can signal how one sides on the issue of reform but more, how it's also a way of taking action in the world.[1] As the conversation continued, exploitation of labor wasn't avoided. There was a recognition that the products and services we have purchased may have been cheaper because the

---

[1] http://www.npr.org/blogs/itsallpolitics/2013/01/30/170677880/in-immigration-debate-undocumented-vs-illegal-is-more-than-just-semantics

workers who produced it weren't paid a fair wage or given proper benefits. How much higher would your grocery bill be if we paid the workers who produced the food that fills our cart a fair living wage? Consumers and corporations benefit from exploiting undocumented immigrant labor.[2]

It's safe to agree that many complex issues contribute to an increased entry of immigrants into this country. Some come to live in freedom and some come and stir up trouble, but every group can be charged with this, legal in this country or not. The truth is that anything surrounding immigration and involving undocumented immigrants will be prevalent in my thoughts and my speech because it is my history. While I may not ever share the perspective of people who are so challenged, people who feel endangered or threatened by us undocumented migrants, I accept the anxiety that comes with the conversations because it allows me to further cultivate my ethical voice and with differing perspectives, I am able to share the brave story of my parents.

By: Hermila Duran, MBA 2014

---

[2] Sociologyinfocus.com. The Power Behind "Illegal Immigration."

MEXICO

For any slight ailment, my mother had an herb or a dried plant in which she would make tea from, reminding me her great grandmother taught her grandmother, and like that, was passed down to her. It always came from a wrinkled plastic, reused bag she would pull out from the same drawer. I probably couldn't name most of them, but some images of these dried plants are unforgettable. The scariest to this day are hairy twig-like pieces, slightly resembling tarantula legs, that she still turns to when anyone so much as alludes to a stomach ache. It reminds me of the well-known use of Windex in My Big Fat Greek Wedding movie[3]. I've since seen and learned how culture informs behaviors, how it transmits knowledge from one generation to the next[4] and how rich and valuable this is.

During group discussion in class, I recognized my challenge out loud: my experience with multinational corporations in Mexico carries such disapproval because I fault these corporations for contributing to changing the culture I strongly identify with. Regardless of whether a company understands the possibility of this, invariably, the western influence happens. Do corporations have a duty to recognize their impact on foreign societies? As I mature, culture has become an increasingly significant contribution to my perspective of the world and when multinationals impose themselves on fragile communities, my biggest challenge lies in the loss of culture and how impactful this is.

In the case of my experience with Brenda, my cousin, the cultural shifts were very western. Why do we believe that the way the US does things is the only way possible? I often find this country to be so unapologetically ethnocentric. [5] After expressing my perspective, I was met with, "what about what a company brings—technology, jobs skills? The struggle of seeing the culture lost is so disheartening that I haven't given this side of the argument much thought, frankly. I'm afraid that losing culture is more significant than corporations care to even think about.

A recent Rick Steves Podcast ignited the injustice again. He interviewed photographer Phil Borges about his work capturing indigenous tribes throughout the world. It was said there are "6,000 languages in the planet; half of them have no children speaking the language. When language goes away, so does culture. In a generation, cultural diversity is going away. Who/what

---

[3] http://.imdb.com/title/tt0259446/quotes
[4] Merriam Webster dictionary
[5] http://www.princeton.edu/~achaney/tmve/wiki100k/docs/Ethocentrism.html

protects cultures?" (Podcast). Again, corporations aren't responsible for saving the world, but I insist mindfulness is lacking. Who threatens these cultures? Phil Borges argues that people want their resources. This struggle for resources is pushed by governments and corporations. It's not the only threat to culture, certainly, but destructive nonetheless[6]. In fact, in chapter 1, Halbert contends that "…developing nations are just learning to want what developed nations have…"[7]

   Abuelito Pedro had a spiritual connection to the land, the type of connection this podcast speaks to, one that sometimes passes as superstition by some. People will say, "They're praying to the mountain god, to the river god…" but this is merely a metaphor. In fact, the connection to the land helps explain and helps us understand our interconnectedness and how we are dependent on all life forms and each other for well-being, development and especially, sustainability. This is the value in culture. From a global perspective, culture carries a powerful unifying bond that results in a global community of sorts that drives behavior and expression, aids in transmitting knowledge. Finally, after more group discussion, it was considered that a changing culture just may be the result of globalization and the world today. While it could be, this doesn't give organizations the right to devalue their place within the cultural structure. Class discussion, conversations and further reading only solidified my stance on the value of culture.

By Hermila Duran, MBA 2014

---

[6] Podcast: Rick Steves, Plight of Indigenous Peoples, 9/8/13
[7] Halbert, Terry. Law & Ethics in the Business Environment. Ch. 1

NATIVE AMERICAN MASCOTS

Native American Mascots in our society is just one of the many issues facing the remaining native population in the Americas. As a group they have one of the highest unemployment levels in the United States today, reaching nearly 15% according to the Bureau of Labor and Statistics 2011 report. What's even more alarming is the fact that nearly 40% of Native Americans living on reservations take home incomes that are below the poverty line. Most people (who aren't Native Americans) assess the wealth of the race based on the casino businesses Natives are so well known for in this country. It really couldn't be any further from the truth. The misconception caused me to research Native American Reservations and the general history of the Natives.

One of my research topics relates very well to the chapter about worker's rights as human rights. As you read the section, you will come across the various examples of slavery that have existed and still do exist in our world today. I knew that European settlers had Black slaves on the very ships that landed in the Americas. What I didn't realize is just how many Native Americans were taken as slaves. I can't help but think I would want to be a casualty of war than to survive as a slave.

The two main reasons why Europeans sailed west were to find a fast trade route to the Asian and Indian lands and gold. As they settled in America they spread disease, murdered and pillaged innocent Native Americans forcing them to either retreat or fight. During this time the Europeans also captured thousands of these Native Americans to be used as slave gold miners. Some would remain in North America while others were shipped to the islands to the south. They were perceived to be of equal or lower class than the African slaves. What a terrible past these people have had, yet all I can really recall from my education on the history of the Native Americans is Pocahontas, John Smith and Thanksgiving. The European English education I have received swept these facts under the rug as I was filing my paper cornucopia with fruits and vegetables. It makes me wonder what else I don't understand while reaffirming my position on the rights of these oppressed Americans and oh yeah, Mascots.

I can't believe we are even talking about mascots at this point, but I guess even obvious debates need to be closed hard and to the point. The people who nearly wiped Native Americans clear off this earth are the same people who created our current government and rule our society today. What they did was terribly wrong. To them the earth was flat and whites were a superior race who had the right to own people as slaves. Our attempt at appeasement and reconciliation is to give Natives terrible plots of land and provide tax incentives. Some Natives have found a way to become awesomely successful with these benefits, but most still struggle mightily. Yet we as a society are not willing to remove mascots that are hurtful and insulting to a society that has already endured so much pain and suffering. The mascots in question do not depict an honorable tradition and need to be removed. It shouldn't be a question at all.

By Daniel Waters, MBA 2014

REDSKIN

If you have been paying attention to the kickoff of the National Football League you have most definitely had your eyes on the return of RG3 from his devastating knee injury in last year playoffs. Robert Griffin has had his fair share of headlines, but not nearly as many as one might expect. Instead, many of the headlines in the nation's capital are about the Washington's mascot of 81 years. So what's the big deal with the Redskin?

Nearly every sport team and organization in the United States associates their group with a symbol or Mascot. The groups adopt mascots in the form of animals, plants, historical references, geographical references, and in some cases Native Americans. A few of the mascots I have been associated with throughout my schooling and athletic endeavors are Indians, Spartans, Bears, Cobras, Bandits, Explorers, Pirates, and golden Generals. I never paid much attention to what these mascots meant until a 7th grade assembly at Springfield Middle School in Montgomery County, PA. The school announced that we would be changing our mascot from an Indian to a Spartan. At the time I thought they were just giving us the same mascot as the high school, now I understand the whole truth behind the change. Many Native Americans find the use of their tribes and warrior chiefs as mascots to be extremely offensive. Initially I think about how long the names have been around and just assume keep the names, no one is physically being hurt by these mascots. However, once I stepped back and actually researched some of these mascots, it's plain to see the correct choice in the matter.

When you "Google" the word Redskin you have to go a few pages deep to find something about an actual Native American. One would think that the word was just created for a football team. Sadly, this is far from the truth. The word redskin is an offensive slang word that should be avoided. Essentially, it is the equivalent to using the "N" word. At one point there were some 3,000 Native American teams in this country. We are now down to 900. I'm just fine with taking all of these mascots off the field.

Tradition is something you should look back upon and be proud. Keeping tradition just for the sake of tradition is imperfect and in some cases offensive. The Washington Redskins should own up and make the change to whatever new mascot they choose. I think the Washington Ear Marks sounds good or perhaps the Washington Filibusters. What's the worst that could happen? Ok I'll tell you. A bunch of football crazy tailgaters are going to lose their minds only to forget about it in a few weeks. At that point they will buy a new jersey and the organization will have made millions in apparel sales while doing the right thing. My next greatest fear is that PETA will be the next in line to fight for the rights of all animal mascots....E-A-G-L-E-S Eagles!

By Daniel Waters, MBA 2014

REFERENCES

http://www.merriam-webster.com/dictionary/redskin

http://inamerica.cnn.com/2013/04/04/native-american-mascots-pride-or-prejudice/

UNTITLED

Over the past several decades, the American legislative system has been very proactive in its attempt to prohibit discrimination especially in the workplace. As a second generation immigrant, first generation born in the United States, I am fortunate to have grown up in an America that is moving towards equality across both race and gender. Being both a minority and a woman, I have seen the worst in people in the way that they stereotype and categorize others for being different and often treated them as an inferior. So often that I've been asked, "Do you speak English?" that I no longer take offense to such questions. Having read of a time before such legislations were passed, I have been able to count my blessings and understand that my reality today could have been much worse.

The first time I was made aware of discrimination in the workplace was in my 12th grade Advanced Placement History class. The topic of the day was affirmative action. Why was such legislation needed? I argued vehemently against its necessity believing that all individuals should be hired or promoted based on their own merits rather than because of quota a company must meet. However, as I move forward in my professional career, I am very aware of this need. I am reminded every day that most of the time, a promotion is not based on what you know, but who you know. I have been made aware that without affirmative action, a white individual will most likely get a position over a minority, all else being equal. The issue isn't as prevalent as it may have been at one time. I truly believe that America is accepting diversity with at least one open arm especially as more minorities climb up the corporate ladder.

Another interesting legislation that passed was the Civil Rights Act of 1991 which established the Glass Ceiling commission. Usually people associate the glass ceiling with its effects on women in the workplace. However, the glass ceiling has also affected many minorities. The glass ceiling is a transparent barrier keeping women and minorities from attaining top positions in companies. A secondary issue that relates to the glass ceiling is the difference in pay across genders. A commission was assembled to focus on this issue and to help women advance in education as well as in their careers. However, the commission disbanded and the issue is still present today.

In addition to the glass ceiling, women are faced with another issue that can be blamed as factor that hinders growth in the workplace and that is the "maternal wall." The maternal wall is a way of describing subtle discrimination against women who become mothers. A "good mother" is a woman who is always available for her kids (Halbert, pg. 151) so she may only work part time or takes more time off than the average worker. She, then, would only be considered an adequate worker which can explain the difference in pay as well as the inability to climb up the corporate ladder. As Jack Welsh stated, "There's no such thing as work-life balance ... There are work life choices, and you make them, and they have consequences." However, as the roles of mothers and fathers, caregivers and providers, are commingling, I believe that we will eventually see the pay gap decrease and more women in top positons.

There isn't any doubt that there is still a long road ahead to equality for both women and minorities. As demographics in all areas continue to become diversified, people are more accepting of other individuals and color plays a smaller role in everyday life. Unlike decades ago, things are becoming less black and white and more of different shades of grey. The government will continue to play a big part in integrating equality but an individuals' persistence to learn and thrive will determine where they land on the social and corporate ladders.

By Saroun Sam, MBA 2014

REFERENCES

Halbert, Terry and Elaine Ingulli. Law & Ethics in the Business Environment 7th Edition 2012.

UNTITLED

The reading focused on valuing diversity, diversity in race, culture, religion, mental or physical abilities, heritage, age, gender, sexual orientation gender identity, etc. Workplace diversity is important because it can provide benefits such as improved moral outside-of-the box thinking, greater teamwork, and an atmosphere of mutual understanding and respect.[1] I have had a first-hand opportunity to see the Equal Opportunity for Individuals with disabilities (Americans with Disabilities Act) in play and how this diversity positively impacts the workforce.

I work at a government agency where all of the cleaning staff is developmentally disabled in one way or another. Working at the agency I've come to learn that they are the best workers and bring so much energy to the workplace. They always have a smile on their face and are always happy and willing to do whatever you ask of them. You could be having the worst day but you pass one of them in the hallway and they smile and say hello or they are emptying your trash with a smile on their face and want to talk about anything under the sun and it instantly brightens your mood. They are also the most loyal workers. In the seven years I've worked at agency I rarely see a new face; the majority of them have been working the same job for 20 plus years. I believe many of these individuals increase the morale of everyone in the workplace and increase production at the same time.

The book talks about the social benefits to society in hiring disabled workers. The book states, "integrating persons with mental disabilities into the workplace creates a society-wide social benefit by helping to erode existing prejudices and misconceptions regarding the group."[2] I find this to be very true in my experience. Prior to having the privilege of working near this diverse group of people I believed that they weren't capable of holding a job, were depressed over the fact that their life wasn't "normal," that they didn't have a breadth of knowledge, and that they couldn't hold a conversation just a name a few. Working around the disabled for the past seven years has erased all of the original misconceptions I had about this group of people. It never ceases to amaze me all of the knowledge that they have, the insights they provide on everyday matters, how truly happy they are and how they don't see their disability as a negative, and how loyal they are. When I pass by those

---

[1] USF.edu. Chapter 12: Managing Diversity in the Workplace. Web. 23 September 2013. http://ucsfhr.ucsf.edu/index.php/pubs/hrguidearticle/chapter-12-managing-diversity-in-the-workplace/

[2] - Halbert, Terry and Elaine Ingulli, Law & Ethics in the Business Environment, p.160 (2012).

with developmental disabilities outside of work now I see them in a different light; I see them as contributing members of society that enjoy the same things that everyone else does. They are people who like to laugh, learn, bring happiness to others, and want to be like for who they are just like everyone else.

I work for the federal government who supports many disabled groups. Where better to start changing people's minds and perspectives on those with disabilities than the government. Not only does our agency hire people with developmental disabilities to handle the cleaning of the facility they also give preference on contracts to agencies that hire those with disabilities. I recently awarded a long-term contract worth $10 million to New York City Industries for the Blind. I never knew the capabilities of those with disabilities until I started working for the government. I have learned a lot about the importance and value of diversity thanks to my job.

Diversity is important in the workplace from both a creative and productive standpoint. This includes those individuals with disabilities. Many people with disabilities are gifted and talented, intelligent, honest and have charisma. They are focused, dedicated and loyal people who will have a positive impact on all of those around them as well as the organization as a whole.

By Jessica Shaeffer, MBA 2014

RACISM

In my opinion, racism is the deeds and the beliefs that underestimate a person's value that he/she belongs to a race or a religion or a different race. It is also used to describe those who believe that the type of transaction with other human beings must control the work of a person's background recipients of such treatment, and that the good treatment should be limited to a certain class without true background that a certain class or must have to the right in control over the lives. The fate of other races Portal was the first acts of racism its prevalent are the slave trade, which was usually practiced against African Americans. There are contemporary examples of racism, such as, racist movements against the Japanese in America during World Wars and Anti-Semitism against the Jewish movement in Europe specifically in Germany and the racism against Middle Easterners and Muslims after the events of September 11.

I am a Muslim and I believe in what is right and wrong. I realized that I only get discriminated against when I'm around the people who are not fully educated. Nevertheless, I never felt less of my religion, my culture or myself when I am around people who are knowledgeable and well informed for whom I am.

The phenomenon of racism must be addressed more often. It is important to understand the roots of racism and the psychological means that stand in the social basis of this phenomenon. There must be knowledge of the phenomena of racism that should be spread in the country; all of these must be of the responsibility of each area. There is a daily need to deal with this phenomenon. Forms of racism affect the multicultural, varied and democratic society that respects human rights of this phenomenon.

By: Alanoud Alobaid, Class of 2016

IN LIVING COLOR: AN ANTHOLOGY

TRANSCENDING THE TRAP OF TRIBALISM

On March 3, 1991, African American Rodney King was brutally beaten by four white police officers. King was pulled over for speeding and then yanked out of his car, before they began to abuse him. This beating was recorded by an over-looker and exposed to the media. The four policemen were then placed on trial, but were acquitted. This verdict created an outburst of riots in Los Angeles, causing fifty-three deaths, numerous injuries, and over one billion dollars worth of damage. Anna Deavere Smith later composed a play, *Twilight: Los Angeles, 1992*, compiling a variety of different people's points-of-view, expressing their feelings on the event and allowing them to say their *side* of the story. Her play focuses on the issue of tribalism, illustrating how people group one another into "tribes," and portrays this effect on a community. In her play, Smith asks directors to have actors play roles that are not necessarily their "type." In her own film, Smith puts on a one-woman show in which she plays all the roles. Her choice of including certain people's interviews juxtaposes the different perspectives people had. Smith uses the actual acting style of her play, along with the different people's interviews, to reveal the play's message on how society needs to stray away from this idea of tribalism and stop separating one another into these groups.

Twilight: Los Angeles, 1992 paints the perfect picture of a community struggling with the issue of tribalism. Tribalism is the state of grouping people into "tribes," or categories. People group themselves based on appearances, beliefs, or on things that they share the same interest or dislike in. In Smith's play, the community of Los Angeles groups themselves mainly through appearances and occupations. After hearing the verdict of the Rodney King case, many African Americans started rioting against it. An anonymous talent agent describes his experience on the day that the Beverly Center was burnt down. He recalls someone asking, "Did you hear *they* are burning down the Beverly Center?" (90). The connotation of the "they" illustrates how African Americans are all grouped together. It doesn't matter if one was sitting at home and not partaking in any of the rioting, if someone was black, they were a part of this "they." People also grouped each other through occupations, especially if one was a police officer, then they were thought of as a notorious cop by many. Rudy Salas, a Mexican-American sculptor and painter, recalls in his interview the one time cops brutally beat him and "from that day on" he says, "I had a hate in me" (30). Salas continues to explain that when he reads the newspaper and hears about a cop that was killed, he doesn't feel sympathy for the "fellow human being" (31). He says, "So you know you know, so what? Maybe he's one of those motherfuckers that y'know…" (31). Although only four policemen abused Salas, he is filled with so much hate that he just jumps to the conclusion that the cop killed was a "bad" cop. Salas groups all cops together and labels them with a notorious stereotype. He disregards the fact that not all cops are actually bad, similar to the way the Los Angeles community completely disregarded the fact that not all blacks partook in the riots. People automatically placed others in "tribes" with a *particular* stereotype just because they had a *particular* look or a *particular* occupation.

Smith's play also portrays how placing one another into different groups created barriers among people and separated the community of Los Angeles. People even became angry if these barriers were broken and one "went against" his own tribe. Stanley K. Sheinbaum, former president of the LA Police Commission, attended a gang meeting. When he went to the meeting, he explains that, "the cops were mad, they were really *mad* that I would go talk to *them*" (27). Sheinbaum wanted to "learn" about them and view things from their perspective, but the rest of the cops did not agree with his act. Sheinbaum continues to explain that he received a letter from a fellow police officer stating, "You-went-in-and-talked-to-our-enemy" (27). The barriers between cops and some of the LA community were so high that cops felt betrayed when Sheinbaum went to the meeting and even referred to the gangs as their "enemy." Shortly after the Rodney King beating, a Korean woman, Soon Ja Du, shot and killed African American teenager, Latasha Harlins, in her store. Charles-Lloyd, "the-top-black-attorney" took on this case and defended Soon Ja Du (42). Gina Rae, an African American community activist who is also known as Queen Malkah, shares her feelings on this case. Rae describes that when Charles-Lloyd decided to defend a Korean, he "sold-his-card" (42). Because Charles-Lloyd was black and defended a Korean, he was viewed as no longer being a part of their "community" (42). Tribalism was becoming so strong in Los Angeles that one could not act out against their tribe in any way without being marked as a trader.

Twilight: Los Angeles 1992 portrays tribalism and its negative effects on society. It also encourages people to stray away from this idea of separating one another and reveals the open mindset that one should have. Smith uses the acting style of her play and the actual words of her interviewees to reveal this message. Smith wants the actors of her play to mostly act a role that is not necessarily their "type" (7). Smith writes, "The theory of the play is that an actor has the ability to walk in another person's 'words' and therefore in their hearts" (7). Having actors play a part that does not match up with their ideal type breaks down the barriers people build up. Smith interviewed more than two hundred people when preparing to write her play, but she only includes certain interviews. Her choice of people portrays the event through different perspectives, but more importantly uses their verbatim words to make her point to stop tribalism. In Sheinbaum's interview, after mentioning the hard time he was given for attending the gang meeting, he asks, "Why do I have to be on a side?" (28). Sheinbaum's question should be a question all people ask. There should be no need to be on one side versus another, rather one should walk on both sides and try to see both perspectives. Reginald Denny, a white truck driver who was almost beaten to death by a group of black men during the rioting, reiterated Smith's message on tribalism. In his interview, Denny says, "I just want people to wake up, It's not a color it's a person!" (115). Denny is right; it doesn't matter what a person looks like, if they're white, or black, or yellow, or brown, no matter the color, they are a human being – someone who deserves justice and equal rites. Smith ends her play with the interview of Twilight Bey, organizer of Gang Truce. Bey explains that, "I can't forever dwell in the idea, just identifying with people like me, and understand me" (171). Bey's statement single-handily illustrates Smith's whole point on tribalism. People need to stop separating themselves into groups and stop secluding themselves with only these people and their specific views.

The Rodney King case and riots affected the community of Los Angeles in a negative way. It sparked the vicious attitudes and prejudices groups held against one another. It also revealed just how strongly people were attached to their own tribes. Anna Deavere Smith takes these devastating events and uses it to portray a message to all people through her play, *Twilight: Los Angeles, 1992*. Through the acting style and interviews she incorporates into her play, Smith makes it very clear how society needs to stray away from this idea of tribalism. She illustrates how one must not build up barriers, separating themselves from other groups, and how we should always try to view things through other's perspective instead of strictly sticking to their own.

By: Cassidy Flanigan, Class of 2018

REFERENCES

Smith, Anna Deavere. *Twilight: Los Angeles, 1992*. New York, NY: Dramatists Play Service, 2003. Print.

QUESTIONS

UNIT 4: Prejudice and Discrimination: Beyond Black and White

1. How do the readings in Unit 4 challenge readers to engage with race "beyond Black and White"? Is this a useful lens to through which to consider race? Why or why not? Use specific examples from texts or artwork to support your point.

2. In "Transcending the Trap of Tribalism," Flanigan analyzes Anna Deavere Smith's play Twilight: Los Angeles, 1992, a one-woman show based on Deavere Smith's interviews with Los Angelenos about the Rodney King verdict and its explosive aftermath. (This anthology contains multiple papers that engage with this provocative play.) Flanigan quotes a character named Twilight Bey, whose portrayal closes the play. Bey says, "I can't forever dwell in the idea, just identifying with people like me, and understand me." How does Bey's line connect to the views of the other characters that Flanigan discusses? How does it connect to the other pieces in the unit? Use specific examples from texts or artwork to support your point.

3. Sam analyzes the issue of "glass ceilings" in education and employment. What is a glass ceiling? What kinds of glass ceilings do we see other writers in this unit grapple with? Use specific examples from texts or artwork to support your point.

4. Coleman's artwork in this chapter is entitled "Jim Crow Lives." What are the key components of this image? How do they connect to the title? Choose one other piece from this unit and explain how Coleman's imagery links to a key idea in that text as well. Use specific examples from texts or artwork to support your point.

5. In Duran's essay "Mexico," the author suggests that corporations pose a threat to the way in which cultures transmit knowledge from one generation to the next, posing the question: do corporations have a duty to recognize their impact on foreign societies? How would you respond to this question? What can corporations do to ensure that they don't negatively impact native cultures?

UNIT 5

Overcoming Bias: Confronting and Confirming

In Unit 5, students explore questions of bias and positionality. Some of the texts call out the biases of others. Some confront the biases held by the authors themselves, their families, or their friends. Some texts level accusations of bias against others without acknowledging their authors' own biases. Unit 5 is provocative and likely to push readers' buttons. The texts in this section are passionate, but not always well-informed; they are personal, but not always conscious of how one person's experience may differ radically from another's. Unit 5 offers opportunities for readers to analyze bias and a valuable lesson in the ways in which we may be blinded by our own.

A "POST-RACIAL" UNITED STATES?

After reviewing the material in "Valuing Diversity" from the text by Terry Halbert and Elaine Ingulli entitled Law and Ethics in the Business Environment, the concept discussed on page 133 of a "Post-Racial" United States drew my attention. In the wake of recent events such as the Michael Brown killing by police in Ferguson, Missouri and the similar Eric Garner case in New York City it is very hard to accept the fact that America is now or ever can be an environment that is truly "void of racial preference, discrimination, and prejudice" as the concept of "Post-Racial" is described by the text.

Despite the fact that certain legislative achievements have been made over the years in this country, starting with the Civil Rights Act of 1964 (Halbert & Ingulli, 134) we are unfortunately still at a point where indirect policies and socio-economic conditions in this country continue to negatively impact minorities. From a legislative and judicial standpoint, we are going to have to make a step change to enact and enforce laws in the true spirit of the Equal Protection Clause within the fourteenth amendment of the Constitution (Halbert & Ingulli, 130). Many states have had the courage to use the Equal Protection Clause as the basis for judicially determining that certain practices such as banning same-sex marriage violate this clause because they not only infringe on fundamental freedoms of individuals, but have both direct and indirect impacts that lead to non-equal social or economic conditions for a minority group.

Cases such as "Lozano v. City of Hazelton" (Halbert & Ingulli, 131) illustrate the inconsistent manner in which states and the federal government have interpreted the Equal Protection Clause over the years. In this case, anti-immigration laws enacted by a city were upheld because "no evidence indicated that the ordinances were approved because of their potential discriminatory impact." This ruling ignores the fact that in reality the ordinances do have a very clear and direct discriminatory impact on a group of both illegal and non-illegal persons of Mexican and Central American descent. Focusing the ruling on the intent of the ordinances as a justification to keep them, while ignoring the actual impact or consequence of them creates a dangerous precedent for enforcement of law that violates the fundamental freedoms of large groups of individuals.

Not all case law has defended the point or taken the stance of the 2007 Hazelton case. The issue is that there simply is no consistency in rulings on these matters. According to Halbert and Ingulli, "while 41 states have adopted some kind of immigration laws," such as Arizona's very aggressive legislation in 2010 (Halbert & Ingulli, 132) others have moved in the opposite direction. Citing examples such as in San Francisco and Trenton, they share examples of cities which have enacted laws to "make life easier for immigrants" through the establishment of community identification cards to provide access to services and places that require identification.

Ultimately when it comes to the Equal Protection Clause, both the judicial and legislative systems in this country will have to enact and defend laws that consistently rule based on the true impact (greater good concept) if we are to truly move any closer toward a "Post-Racial" society in this country. Enabling practices that create inequalities in poverty rates, income levels, home ownership and employment rates (Halbert & Ingulli, 133) for a variety of minority groups will only further contribute and extend racial divides in this country.

By: Neil Greenstein, MBA 2016

"SHOULDERS"

The poem "Shoulders" by Naomi Shihab Nye is about a man carrying his innocent sleeping son on his shoulders through the rain, and trying to protect him. When diving deeper into the meaning behind the words, I felt that he was trying to protect his child from more than just the rain. As a parent, he wanted to protect his child from the world. I instantly felt connected to this poem because I am a single parent, raising a son in a cruel world and I'm constantly trying to protect him as well; protect him from life's disappointments, heartaches, and inequalities. This is a constant struggle for me because in all reality, outside of the four walls of my house, there's only so much I can protect him from. However, I will always have a burning desire to keep him safe at all costs.

I read this poem to my father because I was extremely interested in his perspective. Since I'm the youngest of seven, I was certain he too could relate to the father protecting his "fragile children and handling them with care." I was right. He shared with me his feelings about going to the end of the world and even laying down his life for the protection of his kids. I remember one time when I was in the 3rd grade, a boy in my class stabbed me with a pencil. My dad came up to the school during gym, and threatened to smash the boy's head into the wall if he ever came near me again. He did this in front of the entire class, including the teacher. Needless to say, I've never had any more trouble out of him ever again.

When I read this poem, I thought about some of the current events in the media today and my perspective intensified. Michael Brown, an 18-year old black unarmed teenager was fatally shot in Ferguson Missouri by a white police officer. One hundred days after his death, his murderer was found not guilty. A similar tragedy also occurred two years prior when Trayvon Martin, a 17-year old black unarmed teenager was gunned down by a neighborhood watch volunteer George Zimmerman (Zimmerman referred to himself as a White Hispanic). Here you have two scenarios where justice was obviously not served. As a mother trying to raise a black man, my faith in the justice system is now crippled. It is extremely hard for me to accept that not one but two unarmed teenagers' deaths can be rightly justified. What's worse is the anguish the parents are experiencing due to feeling they failed at protecting their babies. My greatest fear, God forbid, is not being able to protect my child. If I teach my son how to walk away, I fear that he might get stabbed in the back. If I teach my son how to run, it'll never be faster than a speeding bullet. If I teach him how to fight, I have to hope that it's good enough to defend himself, but not too well that the other boy seeks revenge. If I teach my son how to shoot, I'm only going to be perpetuating the violence. I can't trust the justice system because in my opinion, they're crooked as well. This world has become one of labeling each other, and unfortunately, it's not helping the cause. No, not all cops are bad, and no, not all people are racist; I understand this, but not all black men are criminals either, and they need to stop being treated as such.

From my experiences, laws that should be applied to everyone across the board, no matter what race, color, creed, or profession, are evidently not equal. Trayvon was shot and killed because Zimmerman said he looked "suspicious"; suspicious because he's black and was walking in a suburban neighborhood at night with a hoodie on. Why is someone suspicious for wearing a hoodie to protect themselves from the rain? How is self-defense a plausible alibi for someone to bring a gun to a fist fight that they ultimately provoked? And how do you tell those working with our justice system, which has as its main purpose to control crime and impose penalties for violations of the law, that they are acting both illegally and unethically? You can't. It's sad that every black male, whether he's a law abiding citizen or not, is viewed as a thug or criminal all because of the color of his skin. My heart breaks for the mothers who have had to do the unspeakable and bury their sons due to senseless violence. It's a crazy world that we live in. There's a long road ahead of us to recover from all the inequalities of a system that feels like it was never built to protect us. Although the system is supposed to be about right vs. wrong, it seems to be about color. It's appalling how we can all place our right hands over our hearts and pledge allegiance to the same flag and utter the words "one nation, under God, indivisible, with liberty and justice for all" and clearly not mean it. Dr. Martin Luther King Jr. quoted that a riot is the language of the unheard. As we've seen on the news the most recent riots after the Michael Brown murder, people are fed up with not being heard, thus they are now acting out. I know that violence begets more violence, but just standing still and allowing ourselves to fall victim to injustice doesn't feel right either. The poem concluded that the rain will never stop falling. I agree. I just wish I had a raincoat sufficient enough to protect my son from it.

By: Mahasa Taylor, MBA 2015

UNTITLED

I was raised Catholic in a small town in South Jersey. Growing up, I lived a very sheltered life, and did not experience much outside of my home area. My father and grandfather were very close-minded and in some ways prejudiced, though I am embarrassed to admit that. My father was very strict with my sister and me; he would have kicked us out of the house if we dated someone of a different race or the same sex.

As I got older, I had the opportunity to begin to experience life outside my comfort zone in south Jersey. I went away to college and fell in love for the first time. I learned a lot from my first boyfriend; his mother was a lesbian and her girlfriend lived with them. Me being the naïve little girl from the country, did not even realize that they were a couple at first. After a few meetings, I caught on. My boyfriend's mother had dated a man years ago, but eventually started dating this woman soon after he was born. My boyfriend didn't know any other type of family, but was teased and ridiculed in school growing up. Despite some of the difficulties with teasing and bullying, my boyfriend was well-adjusted and normal. His parents loved him just like any other parents. And made sure they gave him the best life possible. He grew up to be a wonderful person and I think his parents played a key part in making him the person he is today.

My then-boyfriend's family structure was my first experience with the gay community and lifestyles. Seeing the love and stability in that family seemed just as normal to me as any other family with a husband and wife as parents. Since then, I have developed friendships with people of all sexes, races, and sexual orientations. I do not look at people for what they look like, or what lifestyle they choose to participate in.

I strongly believe that everyone should have the equal right to marry, whether of the opposite or same sex. What truly matters is the love between two people. If those two people can provide a loving household for children, they should be able to do that. Homosexual couples should be able to marry and be provided the same benefits as heterosexual couples, such as medical, social security and tax. These beliefs are against my Catholic religion, but I think the world we live in has changed, and laws around marriage must change to. I would support any gay couple who chooses to marry.

By: Laura Bider, MBA 2014

RACE TALKIN' IN PRIVATE

In modern America today, it is near impossible to have any societal interactions without the factor of racial relations, between the majority and minorities, to key into them; thus this creates an atmosphere of people awkwardly trying to watch what they are saying in the company of others so that they don't show to be politically incorrect, discriminatory, or, at the worst, racist. In other words, for many years prior the conversations and topics of race relations were ones that were hidden away, but recently they have been more forthcoming in everyday talk. Unfortunately, or rather for this study fortunately, people, when in more comfortable and familiar circumstances, drop their sense of protectiveness and allow for free flow of thought, with regards to race relations, into their conversations with friends and family. In order to access this type of conversation, I allowed myself to be open in three very distinct scenarios in everyday life: driving around, around friends at school, and camping with some of my family. Although all of these scenarios are different with various people, they all produced the same results. The comments and beliefs held by those who were in these scenarios have been formed from their own personal experiences and situations. The point of this essay is to compare the data that I retrieved from these three scenarios to the data that is provided in polling and research done.

Possibly the most interesting comments came from when I went camping with some of my family, where it was just all uncles and nephews; consequently, it created an environment of trust, relaxation, comfort, and manhood. This is important to note since it allowed for the social barriers that we create to come down, thus insuring the free flow of thoughts, ideas, and comments into the discussions that would take place. Some of these are just downright racist things to be said, simply put. One example is when my cousin, an Eagle Scout in the Boy Scouts, was trying to rig a rope going from one end of the campsite to the other, and one of my uncles made a comment towards him, "don't go nigga-rigging it now!" Later on, another uncle was talking about how to clear all the leaves out of his area so that he could pitch his tent, and he said that, "I should have brought a damn Mexican leaf blower … would have made life easier for me." This comment is in reference to the gardener that he has hired several times to do his yard. In order to properly try to understand where these comments came from, one must understand my uncles' background with minorities. They all grew up in South and South-West Philly, almost always being the only white family in the neighborhood; consequently, they were bullied and picked on everyday as the minority of the area. At one point, the surrounding neighborhood boys, who were all black, would throw bricks through my grandmother's house to tell them to leave the neighborhood. Consequently, my uncles were always in fights in order to defend their sisters and their house from being attacked. When they got older, they moved outside of the city and into the suburbs.

As a direct result of this background with interactions with minorities, especially blacks, they have formed this solid and unwavering opinion that most blacks are lazy, free-loading, and trouble starters. Although their opinions are going to be hard to change because of their past, some statistics suggest otherwise. According to the Census ACS 2012, the employment rate for African Americans is around 51%, which is 7% lower than the national average; although, more than "20% of the Black working population over 16 years old are employees of the federal, state, or local government, which is just over 5% higher than the national average. On the other end a much smaller percentage of African Americans are self-employed (3.6%) than the national average of 6.2%" (African American Employment, 2014). When my uncles did decide to move out of the city and into the suburbs, they were also making the choice to move into more segregated living. According to statistics, "four out of five whites live outside of the cities and 86% of whites live in neighborhoods where minorities make up less than 1% of the population. In contrast, 70% of blacks and Latinos live in the cities or inner-ring suburbs" (RACE – The Power of an Illusion).

One of the primary environments that I took advantage of was here at La Salle University, since it offers such a diverse population of students, staff, faculty, and off-campus neighbors, who don't have a direct relation to the university. Living on campus has allowed me and the fellow students to see how the university life clashes with the plight of poor urban living that is inhabited almost solely by a minority black population. While La Salle's student body is still majorly white, there is still a decent amount of diversity within. As recent research has told us, there has been an increase in the amount of minorities going to higher educational institutions. From 1976 till 2011, the amount of African Americans in college has jumped up from 10% to 15%, and Hispanic students from 4% to a total of 14% (U.S. Department of Education, 2013). Unfortunately most talk and race relations topics are saved for inside classroom lectures or debates, jokes about each other's standing in class, or as in one case: when a panel discussion erupts. Earlier into the semester there was a panel discussion that took place in the Dan Rodden Theatre called Black Girl Dangerous. During the discussion there was an altercation between the author presenting, an African American women, named Mia McKenzie, and a student panelist, resulting in McKenzie walking off stage and later assaulting La Salle University on social media. This is an example of a situation where an academic discussion and debate was taken too personally and the topic of racial relations hit too deep.

Although the student population is decently diverse, the off-campus population doesn't reflect this, since the year-round population is almost 100% black, with an average age of 34 years of age (City-Data, 2014). Interestingly I found that, although students give the locals a bad reputation, it is the students that partly give the area a bad reputation and are the ones that cause most of the problems with in the neighborhoods surrounding La Salle. For instance, on several occasions when I have been walking around at night, I have always found the locals to be the ones being the nicest and always looking after me and giving me warnings to stay safe; while, the students, who live off-campus, are the ones being loud, drunk, and starting fights. The tension between the locals of the area and the students is one that can be cut with a knife, meaning that both sides are sick and tired of the other side, but are reluctant to take any action, except for the occasional 9-1-1 call to deal with unruly parties. This is even true at La Salle's favorite drunken stop at night, Happy Fortune. On more the one occasion, my friends have asked me if I wanted "to go get some cat to eat," as a reference to wanting to eat from a Chinese place. This intensifies in their drunken stages, when they are trying to order food in person, while shouting racial slurs to the cashier. Interesting enough, most of these students creating the problems and shouting the racial slurs, at night, are the ones that are saying that it is the locals who are the "racists" and "assholes," by the day. Granted that Olney neighborhood in Philadelphia doesn't have some of the best crime statistics, with a total of 811 reported incidents in the past half year, but how many of them have been caused, or can be traced back to, students that live off-campus (Philadelphia Crime Map, 2014)?

The final scenario that I chose to observe was while in the car driving, whether I was one driving or just a passenger; since, I have found that while the driver is focused on the road, they might not put as much detail into what they are saying, thus creating a more open dialogue between him/her and his/her passenger. When I was driving around at night, I had a friend in the passenger seat and the following comment was said, "Watch out for the blacks, they are harder to see at night time." This comment got me thinking since it is a common joke told between people; from a biological standpoint, the statement is most likely true since the darker skin blends into the dark of night, creating less contrast to see. Unfortunately, I feel like most people just use it as an excuse to say a possibly racist comment without having to admit to the blame of saying a racist comment. Almost a week later, I was in the car with a cousin of mine when we pulled up along a car with a black driver, who was listening to the not stereotypical "black music." Suddenly, my cousin stated, "Nothing is scarier than a black man speaking like a white man, cause then you get friendly with them … then they shoot you." When I thought about the comment, several things started to turn inside of my head. Mainly, I feel like my cousin was insinuating that because the black man was listening to "white music," he should be pulled over for safety reasons. I decided to take a look into the relation of car stops by police and race. According to the Bureau of Justice Statistics, "whites (8.4%), blacks (8.8%), and Hispanics (9.1%) drivers were stopped by the police at similar rates in 2008" (Bureau of Justice Statistics, 2008). The discrepancy plays in when a simple car stop turns into more than just a simple stop, it turns into a search: "Black drivers (12.3%) were about three times as likely as white drivers (3.9%) and about two times as likely as Hispanic drivers (5.8%) to be searched during a traffic stop in 2008" (Bureau of Justice Statistics, 2008). This is a fairly large discrepancy to try and account for.

Over the course of this semester, I was forced to be on alert as to what some of my loved ones were saying in everyday conversation, stuff that all seemed normal at the time; but, from an outside perspective it is just down right mean, discriminatory, and racist. There is a discrepancy between what the polling data tells us is true, and what the general population believes and holds true. This clearly comes out in casual conversations with people, in several different spheres of living. And quite honestly, I am surprised and appalled by the nonchalance that this type ignorant racism is treated with.

By: Christopher Berry, 2017

UNTITLED

I have a myriad of feelings, emotions, and conflicting ideas about Title VII and affirmative action. I have held extensive conversations about diversity, its importance, and comedian Louis CK's quip about white's intolerance of "minority entitlements."

> …You can't take people's historic contexts away from them. White people are like, "Come on, it wasn't us!" They want black people to forget everything. ..Every year white people add 100 years to how long ago slavery was. I've heard educated white people say that slavery was 400 years ago. No, it wasn't. Slavery was a hundred and forty years ago. That's two seventy year old ladies living and dying back to back. That's how recently you could buy a guy. And it isn't like slavery ended and then everything has changed…Give them a little time to be cranky… [3]

Still, I also have an overwhelming pang that "reverse racism" is just as bad (really, it would be racism just the same). If I were to apply the framework and motive of Title VII, some of my personal and professional experiences would result in blatant inequality.

I work in one of the most diverse high schools in South Jersey and take great pride in that. Amazingly, these students come from different socio-economic backgrounds from over 10 different countries. Our biggest discipline issues are uniform code violations and gum chewing. Our students are accepting, and I frequently tout how I get to work in "Oz." However, with diversity comes very difficult conversations and decisions with students' parents or board members. Before I continue, our school does change peoples' lives. When faced with the opportunity to go to this diocesan school versus any public school in the school district, our school becomes a dream for many inner-city minorities. The problem I have is when we give scholarships to people because they are minorities which then deprives students who are more worthy of a scholarship because they are not a minority. This is not "equal opportunity." This is what I call reverse racism.

At the time of this writing, it was announced that Cheyney University, a "historically black" college (and if we're looking to end racism, shouldn't phrases like this be eliminated?) will be looking to restart a 33 year old federal civil rights lawsuit … that was settled in 1999.[4] The state gave Cheney $36.5 million for building upgrades, but it has suffered from low attendance and funding. Alumnus Michael Coard said, "We're trying to make sure that

---

[3] Louis CK on The Tonight Show with Jay Leno Show, January 5, 2013.
[4] Snyder, Susan. "Claiming Racism, Cheyney Alumni Threaten Suit. "Philadelphia Inquirer. 23 Sept. 2013

Cheney is treated not just fairly, not just equally, but equitably." Herein lays the problem: Coard's search to not "just" be treated equally is all that Title VII would and should cover. There should be no special treatment for minorities for the sake of being minorities. If (and this is a big "if") what Chancellor Peter Garland said was true, then Cheyney is being treated equally.

Staying in the collegiate setting, I have heard my students say countless times that, "if I were only a black female, I would've gotten into (insert Ivy League school here)." Should we apply Title VII to this situation, and if their feelings are justified and proven to be true, their arguments should hold water and they are victims of the same racism. I realize there are differences between employment, scholarship, admissions, and state funding, but if we truly want to eliminate racism, we need to remember that removing a bad thing doesn't mean we are putting a good thing in its place. We need to work on not just tolerating, but accepting each other.

In a heated conversation with my class about affirmative action, a young black woman (shamefully admitting this: she is my favorite) stood up. I didn't know what was going to happen next, until she began a rant saying that she thought Title VII was "bull****" and that she didn't want to win anything solely because she was black. The idea of her getting something because she wasn't the best or didn't earn it outright infuriated her. I thought about stopping her, but I am glad I didn't. She continued that it also should upset every single person in the room, regardless of color, because it doesn't treat them as who they are: equals and individuals. Rather, it treated them in accordance to what they looked like. We have come a long way from the 1850s and 1960s, and we still have a lot more work to do. But is affirmative action really the right way?

By: Anonymous, MBA 2014

VALUING DIVERSITY

Halbert and Ingulli discuss many ways we as a society stereotype one another on a daily basis, particularly in the workplace, and how the law attempts to encourage best practices. The text focuses discussion on federal laws against discrimination based on race, religion, sex, national origin, and disability. In my personal reflection on these readings, one of the topics that made an impression on me was the idea of a "Post-Racial" United States.

"A Post-Racial America is a theoretical environment where the United Sates is void of racial preference, discrimination, and prejudice" (Halbert 133). Affirmative Action is the notion of ending racial discrimination, of considering all candidates for employment equally regardless of race, which would develop our country into this "Post-Racial America." Although I believe these ideologies were appropriate and crucial steps to ending terribly racist viewpoints prominent in our country's past, I question the goals for the future of the country and the means to such ends.

For example, the text discussed the case of Steelworkers v. Weber, where a highly eligible white candidate with seniority was denied a job because only 7 black and 6 white trainees could be selected, and there simply were no remaining "white spots" left to fill. Additionally, in my personal experience, I've witnessed many eligible white candidates denied jobs at a global accounting company because of the company's efforts to be recognized as one of the most diversified workplaces. I believe at times our society has a focus on hiring minorities, which by that principle alone violates Affirmative Action and the goal of a "Post-Racial" America.

Despite these two cases evidencing "reverse discrimination," I still am not sure what the solution is for our society. Companies should not have a predisposed percentage of minority vs. non-minority employees. However, if companies aren't aware of maintaining a diverse population in the workplace, we could risk companies returning to the terribly biased practices of our past.

I feel that racial discrimination, no matter how many laws are established around it, will continue to be an issue for our country. It's my hope that the future is filled with individuals without any biases, and that employees are hired based on credentials alone, and race, sex, religion, and nationality are not issues. However, in reality I think that the effects of Affirmative Action will continue to take time to be fully effective, meaning that over the next few generations I hope that the number of minority college students will grow, that there are more minorities in the professional workplace, and as a result, hiring practices for companies aren't forced to be a race issue, but rather solely focused on qualifications of candidates drawn from an even playing field.

By: Jessica Runyen, MBA 2015

REFERENCES

Halbert, T. and Ingulli, E. (2012). Law & Ethics in the Business Environment, 7th Edition, Southwestern: Cengage Learning.

QUESTIONS

UNIT 5: Overcoming Bias: Confronting and Confirming

1. The introduction to this unit acknowledges that the readings in Unit 5 are likely to "push readers' buttons." Which reading in this unit made you feel the most uncomfortable? Why? What bias was that writer bringing to the table? What bias might you be bringing to the table that shaped your reaction?

2. Several of the essays in this chapter explore the concept of a "post-racial" United States. As defined by Law and Ethics in the Business Environment, a "post-racial" society is "void of racial preference, discrimination, or prejudice" (133). Based on the readings in this unit (and, if you'd like, in the other units), would you say we live in a post-racial society? Why or why not? Use specific examples from other or artwork to support your point.

3. Assuming we do not live in a post-racial world and that race differentiates us, do you think we should strive to create a society in which we are "color-blind" (seeing beyond difference) or "color brave" (acknowledging and affirming difference)?

4. In "Race Talkin' in Private," Berry examines the differences between what people claim in public (or in polling data) and what they say in private when they perceive themselves to be in a "safe" space. Have you ever had an experience of having someone confide a troubling or offensive belief to you because they thought you shared that perspective? How did you respond? How would you have wanted to respond?

5. Pick one reading for which you would like to be able to respond directly to the author. What would you say, and why?

UNIT 6

Journalism: The Professional as Witness

Journalism serves many purposes. It informs, it analyzes, it investigates, it entertains and, in its editorial role, it opines. But perhaps no role is more important than journalism's role in bearing witness. During the 1960s, it was television that galvanized the conscience of the nation with its graphic images of black children in the Jim Crow South turned back at the school house door and police dogs sicked on peaceful protestors Today, it is citizen journalists, using cell phones, who have borne witness to the death of unarmed black men and women at the hands of police officers. Here, student journalists use the power of witness to share a slice of the black experience in Philadelphia – what it's like to attend a college where only a few professors look like you; how hate speech gets spread through a popular mobile app; the struggle of a black neighborhood to honor its dead; the courage of black women as they come out of prison; the black adopted brother in a multi-racial household; banter about the politics of Donald Trump at black barbershops and hair salons. And then there is the voice of a saint, a Haitian-American who grows the food he feeds to others at a soup kitchen. "Everyone should be a god in their own way," says Altenor Vaval. "Not in the sense of praising you, but to become the creator of everything you do."

FOSTER CHILD IGNORANTLY MISTAKEN FOR A BURGLAR PEPPER-SPRAYED ENTERING HIS OWN HOME

By: John Schatz

Racism in the United States has reared its ugly head again. In Wake County, N.C., an 18-year-old was pepper-sprayed on the back of his neck up to his eyes for trying to enter his own home.

DeShawn Currie, the boy who got pepper-sprayed, entered through the side door of his house, which his mother left unlocked for him. Currie is a foster child of Ricky and Stacy Tyler. The Tylers are white and Currie black. The Tylers' neighbor profiled Currie and assumed he was trying to break into the house.

Three police officers responded to the call. Currie tried to explain who he was which resulted in the officers pointing to photos of the Tyler family and telling Currie he did not belong in the home.

The arguments ended with Currie being pepper-sprayed. The police report states that Currie was threatening and belligerent.

I'm sure he was mad as he was being told that he didn't live in his home and he wasn't a part of his family. However, I find it hard to imagine an unarmed 18-year-old was threatening to three armed police officers.

The incident became a judgment call on the part of the officers and they did not respond proportionally to the possible threat that Currie might have posed.

Currie's mother said, "My five-year-old last night, she looked at me and said, 'Mama, I don't understand why they hated our brother, and they had to come in and hurt him.'" They didn't have to come in and hurt him. They chose to.

Currie's father summed up his feelings on the situation by saying, "Everything that we've worked so hard for in the past years was stripped away yesterday in just a matter of moments."

As of today, there has been no comment from the Wake County Police Department about the incident. As bad as this lack of response is, the department's lack of communication with the Tyler family is even worse.

The three officers at this point have not faced any consequences for their actions, at least not consequences that have been made known to the public.

The story is upsetting in general, but it is also upsetting in that it speaks to experiences I have had. My family is one that fosters and adopts children. The majority of my immediate family in non-white.

There will be dissenters who argue that the police officers acted in a rational manner, but I believe pepper-spraying Currie was a disproportionate response to the 18-year-old being upset at being told he was burglarizing his own home and stealing from his own family.

Growing up, I have seen my siblings be victimized by racism and have seen people struggle with the existence of a cohesive family that is not all the same skin color. Racism in the country is not a reality that everybody is forced to accept.

Racism is not going to go away on its own. The only way to combat it is through dialogue. Just because you wouldn't have called the cops on Currie doesn't mean racism isn't prevalent across the country. There is a societal responsibility to work toward decreasing the amount of bigoted behavior in the U.S. The persistence of racism isn't something you can pass the buck on. The excuse that, "some people are set in their ways" is just that: an excuse.

It wasn't even a year ago that the Republican National Committee released a tweet that read, "Today we remember Rosa Parks' bold stand and her role in ending racism" (pic.twitter.com/uxIj1QmtkU). Despite the Republican National Committee's tweet last year, racial prejudices are still evident in American society. With events like the Ferguson shooting and Currie being assaulted in his own home, policies like gerrymandering and voter ID laws, and with large sections of the population too uncomfortable to discuss racism, the deep ignorance of such a tweet is apparent.

Originally published in The Collegian, October 9, 2014. Reprinted with permission.

YIK YAK APP STIRS CONTROVERSY AT LA SALLE
By Eddie Dunn

On a Thursday night last fall – dubbed "Thirsty Thursday" because it's often a night for student drinking – a crude debate laced with racist rhetoric lit up smart phones around La Salle University, a Roman Catholic school that sits on 133 acres at 20th Street and Olney Avenue in a predominantly black area of Philadelphia.

"I respect the BlackLivesMatter movement and all. I just don't like how they try to say if you're black, your life is automatically harder than that of an Asian, Hispanic, white person. F*** you, said an anonymous post on the popular social media application." Yik Yak.

"Y'all have all this s*** to say about black. People. Worry about yourselves. Y'all races aren't holy saints so don't try to throw shots at us, responded someone else."

"Hey, that's the s*** black people perpetuate. I'm just using your own weapon against you. Black people are always saying blacks can't be racist because they lack power, the original poster answered."

It's all anonymous

There's no telling who posted the remarks on Yik Yak, a relatively new app that allows users within a five-mile radius to post, reply, like and dislike – all anonymously.

But last fall's outburst of obscenity-laced talk about African Americans, which has continued in spurts during recent months, has deeply disturbed La Salle administrators, faculty members and the student-run school newspaper, which editorialized against it. While critics recognize users' right to free speech, they are concerned about the impact of Yik Yak on the school's neighbors and on civil discourse among an undergraduate student body of more than 4,300 students.

"It is indeed true that all are free to post anonymous and often inflammatory remarks on Yik Yak," said James Moore, the dean of students, in an unusual email sent to all students after last November's Yik Yak postings in the run-up to Homecoming Weekend. "But I propose that it is not the best that our La Salle students and community can do."

Alan Wendell, the senior associate associate dean of students, [who monitors] Yik Yak chatter was even blunter: "Yik Yak really caters to the developmentally less-evolved people," he said in a recent interview. "I mean, if you have to hide behind anonymity to say trashy things about other people, how mature are you?"

The unsupported assertions about race on Yik Yak come at a time when La Salle's demographics are dramatically changing. Founded in 1863 by the Christian Brothers, La Salle was established to provide a practical education for the city's working class Catholics, a predominantly white group descended from Irish and Italian immigrants. Today, the majority of the students are still white, but racial minorities now make up about 45 percent of the student body. African Americans, at 18 percent, are the largest group.

The demographic change, which has accelerated in recent years, has been felt everywhere from student activities, which now include an African-American step team, to the classroom, where new courses, such as "Black Religion in America" are popping up.

Anthony Paul Smith, an assistant professor of religion who developed the class, was so upset after last November's racist postings on Yik Yak that he took to social media to rebuff them. "The pushback is important to see, but our black students and Muslim students shouldn't have to put up with this on their campus," he tweeted. Smith, who is white, joined Yik Yak himself so he could offer support to those who have been demeaned, and he urged other faculty to do the same.

"I think we have all been dismayed by the way racism of many kinds, though especially anti-black racism, has been allowed to fester online in social media spaces," he wrote to faculty colleagues. "Nowhere has this been more vile than the anonymous app Yik Yak." Based in Atlanta, Yik Yak entered app stores in 2013 and took on a head of steam the following year as it spread to college campuses across the country. Its developers tout the app as a tool that "instantly connects people to everyone around them so they can share news, crack jokes, offer support, ask questions, and interact freely."

Yik Yak is the most popular app among college students and other millenials nationwide. Many La Salle students have used but most report "downvoting" content that is racist, mysogynist, bullying or homophobic.

Among other things, the app has a "Nearby" feed, which allows users to observe and interact with other users within a five-mile radius of their location; a "My Herd" feed, which allows users to monitor a specific location's feed even when outside the five-mile radius; and an "Explore" section, which allows "Yakkers" to interact within topical feed sections such as presidential candidate debates or college football games.

All posts are anonymous within the local feed and are available for other users to then anonymously reply to the "Yak" and like or dislike it. If a post gets five dislikes, it disappears from the feed. To guard against misuse by minors, the firm has also set up "Geofences" – invisible fences, imposed by GPS location data, which disable functionality of the app on a high school or middle school campus.

In addition, the company says that it uses filters and pop-ups to warn users if they attempt to post offensive language or images including those that are racist, obscene, defamatory, threatening or demeaning to any person or group. If necessary, it can kill user accounts or take down posts. On request from law enforcement agencies, it can also release users' personal information to authorities so they can track down threats of violence.

Guarding against misuse

"Guarding against misuse is something we take incredibly seriously, and we're constantly working to enhance our protective measures," said Olivia Boger, a company spokeswoman.

Even so, Yik Yak continues to cause turmoil on campuses across the country. Over the past year, incidents involving terroristic threats on Yik Yak have been reported at Missouri, Charleston Southern, Fresno State, Penn State, Emory, Texas A &M, Brigham Young and other universities. "I'm going to stand my ground and shoot every black person I see," wrote Hunter M. Park, a student at Missouri University of Science and Technology, who was arrested following his Yik Yak threat.

Use of Yik Yak to bully students has led to suicides or attempted suicide. In late fall, Jacob Marberger, a resident of Cheltenham and a student at Washington College in Maryland, took his own life following a slew of comments posted about him on Yik Yak. Other young people, such as Elizabeth Long, an 18-year-old suicide survivor in Atlanta, said she had encountered posts on Yik Yak encouraging her to kill herself even as she was recovering. "And I'm not the only one," she said.

Petition to get app removed from stores

In response, Long has started a petition campaign on Change.org to get Yik Yak removed from app stores.

Yik Yak can also stir up incriminating gossip. For example, a La Salle student was wrongfully accused in Yik Yak chatter last fall as the probable rapist in a campus sexual assault. Within hours, the student, who asked not to be named for this article, was considering dropping out of school. "People should not use social media to put down one another," the student said. "Especially when one doesn't even know the person and is just going by what they hear."

Sample of racist feed on Yik Yak.

Nobody but the administrators of Yik Yak has any idea how many La Salle students are registered on Yik Yak, how many actually use it, and what they use it for.

But extrapolating from an informal poll he conducted in December among some 90 students enrolled in his three classes, Joel Garver, an assistant professor of philosophy, estimates that about three-fourths of the student body has used Yik Yak at least once and, among those, 86 percent have encountered content they regard as racist, bullying, misogynistic or homophobic. At the same time, some 80 percent of students who said they were somewhat active on the site also reported that they had "downvoted" offensive content.

"I'm not sure what to do with the information, which is both very discouraging (the amount of hateful content on Yik Yak) and somewhat encouraging (the willingness of students to downvote their fellow students)," Garver wrote to a faculty group. "But I wanted a more accurate picture to help understand the nature and extent of the problem."

Quiet on most days

On a typical day, there isn't much conflict on the Yik Yak feed around the La Salle campus. The usual posts are centered on finding a sexual partner, classes, the school's Wi-Fi, or Spongebob Squarepantsquotes. Every once in a while, someone will post a controversial political question: Why are we accepting Syrian refugees when we have thousands of homeless veterans on our streets? Shouldn't we take care of our own first? said one user.

Other times, things can get nasty. On Dec. 7, for instance, the La Salle-area Yik Yak feed exploded with racially-charged posts and conversation that continued for several hours.

Minorities will not be happy until whites are enslaved like blacks were. Y'all want want want want. You never give, said one user.

Isn't it great when we resort to name calling. In 20 years you'll be in chains again, said another.

OP is a racist b****," said one comment.

To which the OP (Original Poster) responded, Aw I'm I? I don't really care. F*** PC bulls*** Can't wait until Trump takes over and puts y'all back where you belong.

Yik Yak and the First Amendment

While administrators like Wendell decry this kind of invective, there is little they can do to combat it without stepping on First Amendment rights. "There may be some legitimacy for people to be talking about this stuff, but this isn't the way to do it," Wendell complained. "What does it say about our community when this is the way we have these conversations?"

Meantime, some students have decided to scrap the app, though not necessarily because of its sometimes racist content. Explained senior accounting major Amir Tucker, "I mean, I downloaded the app. I just thought that s*** was little weird. I got rid of [it] . . . I didn't want to use it." Added nursing major Annie Tran, "I used to (use it) ...not anymore." Said Andrew Sneed, a sophomore communication major: "There was a lot of stuff on there that was really irrelevant to me as a student and as a person."

As for the predominantly black neighborhood that surrounds La Salle, Yik Yak doesn't seem to have drawn many complaints so far. Ken Houston, an African-American resident who serves on a community advisory group to the university, said most neighbors likely aren't aware of Yik Yak because they can't afford the Internet and live in "survival mode." The presence of racism in the community is nothing new, he said.

"Racist comments and deeds are all around us," Houston said. "We are trying to live through them as they hit us."

THE UPHILL BATTLE TO HIRE MORE BLACK PROFESSORS AT LA SALLE UNIVERSITY

By Anthony Fleet and Nicole Paynter

La Salle University economics professor Richard Mshomba, a native of Tanzania, remembers the day well.

He was standing in the hallway outside his classroom on the first day of the semester. An African-American student approached him with a question: "Are you my professor for this class?" When Mshomba said yes, the student jumped with excitement and gave him a hug. "Finally!" the student exclaimed. "Finally I'm going to have a black professor!" Mshomba, the winner of a Lindback Award for Distinguished Teaching, did his undergraduate work at La Salle. After earning his PhD elsewhere, he returned to the university as a professor in 1991.

Since then, La Salle has made some progress in hiring more black professors, but there are currently just eight blacks, including Mshomba, among the university's 245 full-time faculty or 3.3 percent. By contrast, about 18 percent of La Salle's 4,300 undergraduates are African American. Most have never taken a class from a professor who looks like them or who shares important aspects of their life experiences.

Food services, not teaching

"Most of the black people (at La Salle) are in food services," observed junior Latisha Martin, one of more than 700 African-American students on La Salle's campus in a predominantly black neighborhood at 20th Street and Olney Avenue in Northwest Philadelphia.

Martin and other black students at La Salle, like those on many other campuses across the country, say more black professors are needed to serve as role models and mentors; to offer first-hand experience and understanding in classes such as black history; and to break the homogeneity of the faculty demographics.

LaTisha Martin is one of more than 700 black students at La Salle.

"A lot of teachers here are monotone," complained senior accounting major John Duley, an African American student who has never had a black professor. "Same dress, same ideas, same everything." He said a more diverse faculty would expand learning opportunities for all students. "I think it brings different perspectives and adds to what you're learning," he said.

A national issue

The dearth of black faculty at La Salle mirrors the shortfall at other colleges and universities across the country. Most are struggling to diversify their faculties at a time when there aren't that many blacks coming through the PhD pipeline and entering academia. In 2014, for instance, just 6.4 percent of the doctorates awarded in the United States went to African Americans

Experts point out that most of the newly-minted black PhDs are opting for jobs in government, corporations and foundations instead of academia where starting salaries are relatively low. "Black talent is prized," explained Greer Richardson, an African-American education professor at La Salle. "(Black) people are going to other places where they can make money, where their voices are put on a national stage, where they can move their careers forward."

La Salle education professor Greer Richardson says blacks with PhDs gravitate to more lucrative jobs outside academia.

Currently, about half of all black faculty teach at historically black colleges and universities. Those who are looking for positions at universities outside the black-college circuit are often in such high demand that they can command

starting salaries beyond the reach of schools like La Salle, which is struggling to make up a multi-million-dollar deficit.

A call for stepped-up recruiting

"Almost every institution of higher education should, must and has to do a better job in recruiting diverse faculty members. Period. End of story," said Brian Goldstein, La Salle's provost who oversees the faculty. "Our faculty and staff representation needs to be reflective of the students we have here."

Nationally, blacks constitute 9 percent of the country's professors, while they make up 17 percent of all undergraduates, according to the Integrated Postsecondary Education Data System. Locally, just 4.5 percent of the faculty at Temple University is black, while the student body is 12.5 percent black. At Penn State University, 1.6 percent of the faculty is black, while the student body is 4.1 percent black.

Though only about three percent of La Salle's faculty is black, the university was able to add another black professor to its ranks last fall when it hired Baba Jallow, a native of Gambia, as a full-time professor in the school's history department. The department hired its first African-American professor in 1967, ahead of many other schools. He rose to become department chair and retired several years ago.

"I do think that African-American and African professors are under represented on many college campuses, with the obvious exception of the historically-black colleges," said Jallow. "I do not know all the reasons why this is so, but I think many black students would like to see more of their own on college campuses."

Goldstein, who was named just last year as La Salle's provost, hopes to use three strategies to hire more black professors. One strategy, he said, is to make sure that faculty search committees, which look for prospective faculty members, are themselves diverse. Another approach is to set aside special "opportunity" funds that could be used to bring a minority faculty member to campus if an opportunity arises regardless of whether there is a faculty search underway, he said. In addition, Goldstein said that ads for new faculty members should encourage candidates from under-represented groups to apply. Robert Bruce Slater, managing editor of the Journal of Blacks in Higher Education, called for similar strategies. "Make sure they seek out minority candidates and include current minority faculty on search committees," he said. Creating pre-doctoral and post-doctoral fellowships for minority graduate students can also help expand the pool of blacks moving into academia, he noted.

Number one student demand

The lack of black professors became a national conversation last year when the University of Missouri was the first of many schools across the country where black students demonstrated about racial issues on campus. Images of students lining the streets, locking arms and camping in the quad were splashed across the news media. Other schools, including Yale University and Ithaca College, joined in on the protests. In a poll conducted by FiveThirtyEight, a non-partisan polling aggregation website, the number one demand of the protestors at 38 of 51 schools was the diversification of the faculty.

"It says that the students want their institutions to do more to attract black faculty," said Slater. "Some like Brown, Johns Hopkins and Yale have recently initiated multi-million efforts aimed at increasing faculty diversity," he said. "Students want to see a real effort being made and not just talk."

At La Salle, where a major reorganization of academic programs is expected as the school works to get its financial house in order, it's not clear how much faculty hiring will occur in the immediate future. But for many African-American students, the hiring of more black professors can't come soon enough.

Offering "a unique experience"

"I think La Salle should get more black professors," said senior Bianca Desamour, an African-American who is majoring in art history and communication major. "They offer a unique experience and I feel like they're able to offer more insight on cultural norms."

"I don't think I've seen one (a black professor)," said Isaac Perry, a senior who has spent eight years at La Salle working on his undergraduate degree.

Senior Amir Tucker, who is also black, said he felt lucky to have had one black professor during his nearly four years at La Salle.

Amir Tucker says he will "never forget" the mentoring he got from a black professor at La Salle.

"I will never forget him."

"I will never forget him," Tucker said. "I felt like the teacher really cared," he recalled. "He sat down and talked to me about being late and you could tell that he related to me solely because I was African American and doing something good (attending college) that most people my age don't do."

Tucker said that someday, he'd like to be a teacher. "That's one of the things I want to do when I get older," he said. "I want to go back to school and teach other kids who are in my situation."

Getting more black students into the graduate school pipeline and out into college teaching positions is music to the ears to La Salle religion professor Anthony Paul Smith, who is white. Last fall, he offered a new course called "Black Religion in America." The class, which Smith said he organized as a way to teach about the black church as a force against racism and white supremacy, drew some 30 students, both black and white.

"A symptom of the problem"

Early on, Smith told his students that having a white man teach a course on black religion was "a symptom of the problem" of too few black professors at colleges and universities. "It's wrong and it kind of goes against the principles of La Salle that we have such a diverse population and that's not reflected to them in the figures who stand before them in class," he said during a recent interview.

Smith's students, who give him high marks as a teacher, had different reactions to the issue he posed.

Taylor Cammon didn't expect a black professor in her "Black Religion in America" class at La Salle.

"It didn't even cross my mind having a black professor [for this class] because I never had one," said Taylor Cammon, an African American student. "I was like, 'it's my senior year, I'm not getting a black professor now.'"

Suzanne Ramsahai, a biracial student in the class, said a black professor should have taught the class. "He or she can effectively teach black history/studies because of his or her direct connection to the stories and issues that have occurred," she said.

"We come to college to have our preconceived notions challenged," said Alex Palma, a white student who took the black religion course. "Taking this class was a way for me to understand a part of life I didn't know much about."

COMMEMORATING A COLONIAL-ERA BURIAL GROUND FOR BLACKS IN GERMANTOWN

By Germantown Beat Staff
with reporting contributions from Jordan Green '16

More than 260 years after the colonial German Township set up a separate burial ground for "all Strangers, Negroes and Mulattoes," workers have begun planting grass sod at the long-neglected site to commemorate one of America's first cemeteries for slaves and other people of color.

The grass, which covers a parcel of land the size of a football field, sits at the center of a new $22 million low-rise housing complex now nearing completion by the Philadelphia Housing Authority on the block bounded by Queen Lane, Pulaski, Penn and Priscilla streets.

Alex Bartlett, librarian at the Germantown Historical Society, holds copy of document recording the sale of land in Germantown to become one of America's earliest burial grounds for blacks.

The planting, begun earlier in March, is the first concrete step toward official recognition of the site as an historic black burial ground.

Getting respect

For residents in the predominantly black Germantown neighborhood, commemoration of the burial ground can't come soon enough. "I would like to see the site get the respect it deserves as a cemetery for black people," said Barry Leland, 76, a retired Budd Company worker who joined in the successful community campaign to maintain and recognize what came to be known as the Germantown potter's field.

Michael Johns, senior executive vice president for capital projects and development at the Philadelphia Housing Authority, acknowledged that recognition of the potter's field was long overdue. "In the past," he said, "these types of burial grounds weren't given the sort of attention and reverence that they should have received. It's important for a public institution like the housing authority, when we do any major development, to look at the community in which the development is built."

Recovering lost history

The push to find, save and honor the former black burial ground in Germantown is part of a citywide effort by African-American activists and others to recover lost memories of slavery and the history of blacks, both slave and free, in the North.

Copy of cover page from 1755 documenting sale of land for a separate burial ground for "strangers" and people of color.

In recent years, for instance, historians have documented that George Washington held nine enslaved Africans in his house a block from Independence Hall when he was president. Benjamin Chew, a distinguished colonial jurist who built Cliveden House in Germantown, was the largest slave holder in Pennsylvania. Black burial grounds have been uncovered everywhere from Germantown to South Philadelphia.

"Not only are we connecting to the bones of ancestors, but we are also giving rebirth to the stories of people who were denied a history," said George Boudreau, a historian at La Salle University who teaches early American and African-American history. "Imagine being a person who knows your grandmother's bones have been paved over for a parking lot."

The burial ground in Germantown, which is owned by the housing authority, has had a checkered – and controversial – history.

Workers at the new housing site have begun rolling out grass sod in the center of the low-rise complex.

The purchase in 1755

It was purchased by the German Township in 1755 as a separate cemetery for non-residents and people of color. The price: $1 to bury an adult, 50 cents to bury a child. How many people were buried there is not known. Records at the Germantown Historical Society have documented the burial of a "dead negroe child" in 1766. Records also show burials of "W.H." in 1840, "S.H." in 1848 and "John Brown" in 1914.

At the beginning of the 20th century, neighborhood boys turned the potter's field into a makeshift baseball diamond, using headstones as bases. John Brown's tombstone became home plate, according to a 1915 story in the Independent Gazette, a Germantown newspaper. By 1916, the city health department had declared the field a public nuisance, calling it a "desolate spot" full of litter, chickens, ducks, and feral cats.

No more burials were allowed on the site, which was turned into a playground for the Wissahickon Boys Club. During construction of the playground, the tombstones of W.H. and S.H. were unearthed, according to a 1920 press account. There are no records of what happened to the two tombstones, and nobody has ever found the tombstone of John Brown.

A high-rise for the poor

In 1955, the housing authority, which had acquired the land, constructed a 16-story high-rise at the site. Known as the Queen Lane Apartments, the high rise eventually became a tenement ridden with crime and drugs. By 2011, the authority shuttered the building and began making plans to tear it down and construct low-rise housing at the site.

Although many in Germantown were happy to see the high-rise go, the plan to build anew on top of the potter's field drew stiff opposition from neighborhood activists. Unlike the 1950s, when there was little public attention to black history, the residents of Germantown were now up at arms about building on top of what they regarded as "hallowed ground."

They successfully fought the housing authority, winning an agreement from the federal agency not to build atop the burial ground and to commemorate the site with grass and a commemorative marker.

No remains found

Before the high-rise was imploded in 2014 to make way for the new low-rise public housing, extensive archeological studies at the site found no human remains. What happened to the bones of those buried there? Nobody knows for sure. Alex Bartlett, librarian at the Germantown Historical Society, speculated that the remains may have become part of the debris during construction of the high-rise in 1955. Others speculate that the bodies may have been exhumed and moved elsewhere, but nobody knows where.

New low-rise public housing now in the final stages of construction on Pulaski Street in Germantown.

"There was total disrespect," said Leland, the retiree who grew up near the site and delivered newspapers in the neighborhood as a teenager. "The people buried there were disrespected. So what? I feel as though the whole neighborhood was disrespected." Today, the U.S. Department of Housing and Urban Development (HUD) is overseeing a consultative process to determine the design and use of green space at the potter's field, as well as the design and content of a memorial plaque or marker to be placed at the site. The consultation involves representatives from a wide array of public and private organizations, including representatives of Northwest Germantown Neighbors, a community group that led the drive to preserve the potter's field.

Working together on the design

"We want to make sure we are providing something that is in the community's best interest," said Brian Schlosnagle, the HUD engineer who is overseeing the consultation.

He said that brainstorming so far has turned up a variety of ideas for landscaping the potter's field. The ideas include a field for youth to play football or baseball; a leisure park with benches and paths; and community gardens with raised beds of fruits and vegetables.

Schlosnagle said the group is exploring various signage options for a marker of some kind, which it hopes will win approval as a state historical marker. The options, he said, range from a very simple description of the site to a more elaborate history. The group must submit its proposal to the state by next December.

One key issue, Schlosnagle said, will be raising additional funds to finance something beyond the basic landscaping that is now being done at the site. State funds, he said, cover only the basics, and federal funding for the low-rise housing complex have already been allocated. "Right now," he said, "we are exploring different possibilities."

FACE TO FACE WITH ALTENOR VAVAL:
"FOOD IS MORE ABOUT LOVE THAN KNOWLEDGE"

By Amanda Keaton

Walking up the narrow steps into St. Vincent de Paul Roman Catholic Church on Price Street in East Germantown, you will see people sitting outside enjoying the fresh air. Entering through the doors, you will pass others walking in and out of the dining hall, workers getting rid of full garbage bags, and bringing more food out to the guests.

There is one doorway that connects the dining hall to the kitchen, which is where you will find Chef Altenor Vaval, preparing food and dispensing wisdom. "Food is more about love than knowledge," he said. "Knowing how to cook is great. But loving how to do it is more important."

Al, as everyone calls him, is a native of Haiti. He began working as a chef for the soup kitchen run out of the St. Vincent's parish three years ago. Now, he is also director of the dining hall. The free meals that Al prepares are sponsored by Face to Face, a non-profit organization that provides a wide range of services to low-income residents of Germantown, including meals served on Friday through Monday from noon to 1:45 p.m. The organization's motto is: "Hospitality, Mutuality, and Transformation." Al is a paragon of all of these.

It's about learning

Al says that working in a soup kitchen is about learning: learning the ingredients, learning the environment, learning the people, and learning what the people love.

The two rules he has are safety and respect. A clean environment is important so that no one will get hurt in the kitchen. Also if he doesn't have a clean environment, he will make everyone sick and says that no one can afford that.

"I am from a poor country so I understand when someone comes to me and says 'I need food,'" Al explained. "When someone needs food, that doesn't mean I serve them poorly. We are supposed to respect the people we serve and serve them in a clean environment."

Natural, not canned

Not only does Al make sure people are served properly, he tries to make sure the meals are as healthy as possible by using natural food rather than processed food. "The only time I use canned foods is if there is absolutely no fresh stuff," he said. Al's specialty meals are Caribbean and French Cuisine. "But I can make everything," he noted.

Al says being in a soup kitchen is a challenge because 60 percent of the food comes from donation and he can't trash it. Because he doesn't know what is coming, he needs to know how to cook everything.

Learning from family

Al learned how to cook from his grandmother. He says that when he was younger, his siblings would travel for vacation but he would stay with his grandmother and learn how to cook. "We learn everything from family. Everything is about family. My grandmother didn't go to school and most of the things you learn at school is the icing on the cake. But if you put your head on top of your shoulders you can say, 'Wow, I can do that!' School isn't going to teach you how to caramelize an onion."

When Al came to America, he saw that people eat a lot of meat and grease. So when he makes his meals, he uses more vegetables than meat. "When I started working here, I saw that they don't use fresh fruits and vegetables. I think we are everything we eat so I tried to incorporate more fruits and vegetables."

During the summer, Al gets leftover fruits and vegetables donated by farmer markets in Germatown. But now he's started to grow his own in a new community garden adjacent to the church. "I also thought if we can start a garden, we can incorporate it with the kitchen so we can have more vegetables for the people," he said.

Fans speak up

Al, who speaks both French and English, is adored by the regulars at the dining hall. "Al is wonderful and his meals are very tasty, especially his soups," said one seven-year veteran of the kitchen crew. "He's gotten more fresh fruits and vegetables than people know."

Valerie Scott, a Germantown resident, used to help Al prep in the kitchen back in 2013. "He is a wonderful chef. He makes everything from scratch and never turns down a meal if asked to make one," she said.

Scott wasn't a soup person until she tried Al's soup: "He tried to get me to eat squash soup, so I did and it was so good. It is great, especially in the winter." She noted that Al treats his co-workers like family. "He is really about 'doing,' while we're here on earth, to help others," she said.

Carl Weissinger, another kitchen worker, praised Al's attention to serving natural food. "He makes a terrific, tasty, and delicious meal that is all very healthy," he said. Al affectionately calls Weissinger "the German guy." He added, "When you know your roots, you become more grounded and no one can shake you."

Robert Best has been helping out at the dining hall for two years. "Al's ingenuity springs from what is given to him," he said. "I am impressed with his creativity and nourishing way with things he may not know are coming. And the food is always nutritious and healthy."

Al says, "I always invite people to be friendly. If I cook something and they don't like it, I go over, talk to them, and change the meal." Sometimes Muslim people come in so Al has to let them know if he makes pork so that he can make a separate meal for them.

Prepping on Saturday

Saturday is Al's favorite day because it's prep day. "The prep is more difficult than cooking. If you prep the way you are supposed to, it becomes easier to cook it." He even teaches people how to cook when they come in on prep day.

Children are Al's biggest weakness. "When you put children together, they play together. They think about the moment," he said. If everyone could have the mindset of children — and not worry about the past or the future — then society would be the better for it, he said.

Al has plans for the small area outside the church. He wants to create a smaller garden for the children where they can grow their own vegetables and be able to connect with nature.

After studying law in Haiti, Al is currently back in school, taking criminal justice classes at Mercer Community College in New Jersey. He wants to return to Haiti to teach his people about personal transformation and social change.

"Everyone should be a god in their own way. Not in the sense of praising you, but to become the creator of everything you do," he said. Life, he believes, is about creating goodness and greatness in people's lives.

WOMEN: THE FORGOTTEN FACE OF INCARCERATION

By MegAnne Liebsch

Nadine was 19 years old when she was first incarcerated. After that, she spent most of her life in and out of Pennsylvania state prisons on drug-related charges. Today, she's been clean for seven years and is now out on parole, looking to rebuild her life with the help of Sisters Returning Home, a non-profit service organization in Philadelphia's Germantown section. "It's hard to get a job, but I am not a failure," Nadine said during a recent panel discussion at La Salle University. "Just because I made some bad decisions doesn't mean I have to keep giving up on myself."

Nadine, who did not want her last name used, represents the forgotten face of incarceration in America. While public attention has focused on the large number of African-American men who have been imprisoned on drug charges, the plight of African-American women like Nadine has received relatively little attention.

Except for a scattering of programs such as Sisters Returning Home, the criminal justice system lacks gender-responsive treatment for women, experts told the La Salle audience. There are fewer services inside and outside of prison for women. Prison programs, even in female prisons, were designed for men, and after prison, many women are immediately forced to care for their families, often without support for employment or housing.

"Most women who are in prison don't need to be incarcerated," said Jill McCorkel, a sociologist at Villanova University. "They need resources."

More women in jail

Although men – particularly African American men – constitute the majority of those who are incarcerated, female incarceration is on the rise.

The number of incarcerated women in the United States in 2014 was over eight times greater than it was in 1980, a growth rate one and a half times greater than that for men who are incarcerated, according to the federal Bureau of Justice Statistics.

Since 1980, female incarceration rates have been steeply rising. (Sources: U.S. Bureau of Justice Statistics and The Sentencing Project.)

In 1980, there were just 26,378 women in jails and prisons. By 2014, the figure had jumped to 215,332, almost a 10-fold increase. The reason, said

McCorkel, is not that women are committing more crimes. Rather, she said, courts are imposing harsher sentences for drug-related crimes.

In 1986, for example, just 12 percent of incarcerated women were in jail or prison because they had been convicted of a drug offense. By 2014, the figure had jumped to 24 percent.

In the 1980s, women who were convicted of nonviolent crimes, primarily drug offenses, were more likely to be given lighter or community-based sentences, especially if they claimed caretaker status, according to McCorkel. Now, due to mandatory minimum laws, which require convicted people to serve a certain prison sentence based on their crime, more women and mothers are forced to serve sentences in prison. Currently, more than 5,200 women are now incarcerated in Pennsylvania, according to The Sentencing Project, a national advocacy group. And like prisons for men, the two state prisons for women are overcrowded. Cambridge Springs in northwestern Pennsylvania, for example, is operating at 117.8 percent of capacity, according to a 2016 report of the Pennsylvania Department of Corrections.

Sisters offers resources

Sisters Returning Home, located at 304 W. Schoolhouse Lane, is one of the few organizations in the Philadelphia area that helps women after they have been released from prison. The program runs three days a week for four hours. Most women are brought there from halfway houses. "Coming to Sisters changed my whole pattern of negativity," Nadine said. "My whole thinking is changed. I know today I have a choice."

Peggy Sims, director of the Sisters program, said it aims to provide the resources that returning women desperately need. The women take classes to learn budgeting, finance and computer skills. They get help writing cover letters, resumes, applying for jobs, applying for housing and getting in touch with their families. Last year, they went to the circus and had Thanksgiving dinner together.

"It just makes me so happy to come here," said Carol, a 48-year-old woman who has been with the program for three months. "Sisters is a safe haven for women. If I didn't come here, I don't know what I would do." Like others, she did not want to disclose her last name for fear of stigma.

Carol said she was incarcerated for child endangerment because she, her husband and her children were living in a condemned house in South Philadelphia. "I couldn't afford nothing else," she explained. Her children were put in foster care while she and her husband served their sentences. Carol said she has not seen her children since she was arrested, and she will not be able to see them until she has a stable home.

"I hear them in my mind. I see them. I dream about them," she said wistfully. When she thinks about losing her children, she said she sometimes has panic attacks. "But, when I come here," she said of the Sisters program, "they make me feel better. I wish it was five days instead of three days."

The Sisters program also provides recently released women with resources to meet immediate needs –toiletries, feminine products and clothes, for example. Recently, a woman came to the program with only her prison jumpsuit. Sisters gave her clothes and arranged for her to have a room to herself in a half-way house, Sims said.

"They need more facilities for women like this. The women are always way in the back (when getting services)," Nadine said. Once she graduates from the program she hopes to be able to give back to Sisters by donating clothes and toiletries like those that have been donated to her.

Despite the need it fills, Sisters Returning Home has limited openings. The program can only take about eight to 10 women at a time in order to give each woman the attention she needs, Sims said. And for every woman the program serves, there are many more that it can't serve, most of whom are women of color.

Racial disparities According to the federal Substance Abuse and Mental Health Services Administration, black women outnumber white women in prison by nearly three to one despite the fact that the rate of illicit drug use is the same for both races. McCorkel blames biased sentencing. "You can't logically draw any other conclusion," she said.

As the incarceration rate for women continues to rise, more and more children are left without both their fathers and their mothers, Sims said. Often, they live with extended family or, like Carol's children, go into foster care.

When incarcerated women re-enter society, many are barred from receiving welfare. Women returning from prison have difficulty reapplying for programs such as Medicaid and SNAP (food stamps). Most released women cannot get federal housing and other types of government assistance that they need to get back on their feet and avoid re-incarceration.

"When we return home, it's always a hassle to get funding," Nadine complained. Research by the National Institute of Justice indicates that released prisons need programs and services to prevent them from returning to harmful habits. More than 75 percent of released drug offenders, for instance, will be re-arrested within five years of their release, according to the Bureau of Justice Statistics.

In order to prevent such recidivism, Sims said the government needs to step up and provide funding to support women make the transition from prison to civilian life. "They are still valuable to our society," she said. "We sit up here and recycle our trash and throw out our people."

Carol, who was released from prison in 2015, is hopeful of being reunited with her children.

Still optimistic

Despite the challenges, Nadine and Carol are optimistic about their futures. Nadine has recently entered phase four of her release plan with the State Intermediate Punishment program. One recent weekend, she went home to see her family on her first furlough from the halfway house.

With help from Sisters Returning Home, Carol has put in a "home plan" with her parole officer. Once Carol's plan is approved she can move out of the halfway house and into her own place where she can finally see her kids again.

QUESTIONS

UNIT 6: Journalism: The Professional as Witness

1. Most of the articles in this unit were originally published on Germantown Beat, a blog produced by Community Journalism students who research and write in-depth stories on the neighborhood surrounding La Salle University. Based on the articles you've read here, what is the purpose of Community Journalism? How could articles like this help to improve the community? How could articles like this help to improve student understanding of and assumptions about the neighborhood?

2. Many of the pieces in this unit focus on the efforts of local individuals or organizations to create social change in people's lives. In "Commemorating a Colonial-Era Burial Ground for Blacks in Germantown," the community journalists instead focus on efforts to preserve and reclaim history. How does a project like this connect to the other articles in the unit? How does a project like this connect to other articles in the anthology? Use specific examples from texts or artwork to support your point.

3. Al Vaval, the chef profiled in Keaton's article, aspires to return to Haiti "to teach his people about personal transformation and social change." Where do we see those ideas at work in Keaton's profile of Al? Where do we see those ideas at work elsewhere in this unit (or in other units)? Use specific examples from texts or artwork to support your point.

4. How do these pieces help us understand how history and context affect the life experiences of Germantown residents today? If you were planning a community journalism project for YOUR neighborhood, what under-reported history and context would you focus on? Why?

5. Given the acknowledged importance of recruiting and maintaining a diverse group of faculty members, what are some challenges that La Salle and other universities face when attempting to do this? How might you try to address these challenges?

UNIT 7

Hope: Finding the Inspiration, the Tools to Fight On

The texts in Unit 7 offer hopeful reflections on where we go from here. The source of inspiration varies widely, from renowned activists to faith in entrepreneurship to confidence in the effectiveness of government policy in driving social change. Unit 7 provides an opportunity to analyze the relationship between hope, inspiration, and the structural dimensions of social change. One might question whether these sources of inspiration affect structural injustices or whether the activism of a charismatic leader can be enough to spur widespread, grassroots change.

THE URGENCY OF "RIGHT HERE RIGHT NOW"

Can you see the ... suffering, hunger, hardships, major diseases, disparity, poverty ... Can you feel? The oppression, terror, the injustice, the inequality, the discrimination, yet bravery? Crying who will help me with ... warm blankets, books for school, pencils to write with, paper, doctor visits, enough food to eat, transportation, imagination of the future, to believe, to dream. In 2011 a non profit called Feeding America reported that 1 of 5 American children are at risk of not having enough nutritious food; for African American children the statistics say 1 out of 3.

When prepping for the Poor People Campaign in June 1968, Dr. King spoke about shocking statistics around unemployment in the black community. He said that poverty and economic inequalities threaten the future of America's democracy. During that same speech in 1968, Dr. King says, millions of American people finds themselves walking the streets in search of jobs that do not exist.

During his state of the union address on January 28, 2014, President Obama talks about the same issues and he says, "It is time to turn our unemployment system into a reemployment system..." and "It's time to stop rewarding businesses that ship jobs overseas, and start rewarding companies that create jobs right here in America."

Right here and right now the current unemployment rate is 6.7%, specifically speaking for whites 5.9%; for Hispanics at 6%; and for Blacks booming 11.9%. This is evidence that we have not yet solved this problem.

So right here and right now, I would like to present the idea of social innovation and social entrepreneurship. What if I told you this could create jobs while combating hunger and social inequality. Ladies and gentlemen I am basically asking you to take another look at the non-profit sector. We need to stop looking at non-profits as just a place for charitable donations, but as a way of creating opportunities for people to earn a living,

See, in June of 1968 Dr. King had a dream; on January 28, 2014 President Obama had a vision and right now, I come to you with a solution. Yes, I believe that with sound entrepreneurial principles, the power of an enterprise can truly change the world.

I would like to emphasis the urgency for you all to join the movement and make a change, lets improve the quality of life and standard of living. Right here and right now.

By John Sneh, Class of 2014

"THE DRUM MAJOR INSTINCT"
REFLECTION FROM THE SERMON DELIVERED BY REV. DR. MARTIN LUTHER KING, JR.

I would like to thank the community building team of La Salle University for inviting me to reflect on Dr. Martin Luther King's wise words. I will be reflecting upon on one of Dr. King's last sermons titled "The Drum Major Instinct." We are called together this afternoon to celebrate the life and legacy of Dr. King.

Although the sermon was delivered over 40 years ago to his congregation at the Ebenezer Baptist Church, his message continues to uplift us. I'm grateful to reflect upon his work, which continues to inspire the work of my own. In this sermon, Dr. King profoundly highlights the power of servant leadership.

As a Student at La Salle and as President of a nonprofit organization dedicated to improving the lives of others, I realize how important it is to be aware of such an impulse. An impulse in which all of us have. The desire that pushes us to surpass others, to achieve distinction, to lead the parade - the drum major instinct.

When people hear the word leadership, some make assumptions that leadership is a term only to be used for those who hold an office, manage people, or give direction. Let us look beyond the assumption and realize that leadership is not just about managing people or giving direction. Look beyond and realize that leadership is far greater than the assumptions presented. In the sermon, Dr. King provided a reference to the story of sons James and John in conversation with Jesus. The sons made a single request to Jesus. James and John wanted Jesus to select one, to sit on one side of the throne.

Jesus replied to the request and said in substance, "Oh, I see, you want to be first. You want to be great. You want to be important. You want to be significant. Well, you ought to be. If you're going to be my disciple, you must be." But he reordered priorities. And he said, "Yes, don't give up this instinct. It's a good instinct if you use it right. (Yes) It's a good instinct if you don't distort it and pervert it. Don't give it up. Keep feeling the need for being important. Keep feeling the need for being first. But I want you to be first in love. (Amen) I want you to be first in moral excellence. I want you to be first in generosity. That is what I want you to do."

In the coming days, we will see what happens when the drum major instinct is not contained. In a few days, we will experience a new form of leadership. Leadership ignited by hateful rhetoric. This is what leadership is not. Being a leader means serving others, being a leader means helping your fellow neighbor, being a leader means inspiring others to lead. Let us realize that we all have the power to be leaders; we have all have the ability to serve.

By: Kenneth Brewer, Jr., Class of 2017

IN LIVING COLOR: AN ANTHOLOGY
CONTEMPORARY STUDENT VOICES ON RACE

What really causes a human being to mistreat and underestimate another human being to the point that causes someone to lose complete respect for another? Didn't God create all men equal? For some people this is just an allegory, they don't care. They limit themselves by judging and hurting others for the simple fact that they have different backgrounds and different ethnicities. December 1955 was the beginning of a new generation of heroes who protested against injustices and mistreatment that caused slavery and murders of black people by white people (PBS, 2016). This marked the year that America witnessed great African American pioneers such as Rosa Parks and Dr. Martin Luther King Jr., who used a non-violent war to defend African Americans and minorities' rights, causing a great impact that changed the course of our lives in the United States.

It is not surprising that the amazing power of women played an important role in our history. In 1955 Rosa Parks, an African American woman and a member of the National Association for the Advance of Colored People (NAACP), protested against the inequality of human rights because she refused to be discriminated against by having to sit in the back of a bus in Montgomery, Alabama (PBS, 2016). For countless months individuals trudged through the heat, the cold, and the rainy weather with nothing but their own two feet to travel for miles on end, to support freedom. This event promoted the cause of the biggest revolution and motivated others to follow her footsteps by refusing to take buses, initiating a large campaign of walking for African Americans who were demanding the end of segregation by white Americans.

The biggest cause of this revolution began when African Americans were brought to the US not to favor them, but the contrary, to force them to serve as slaves. They were sold as objects in the business market generating wealth created by the white rulers. This event caused in 1966 the appearance of revolutionary groups such as the "black panthers" who considered themselves as soldiers who embraced the same mission to fight for equal rights. Unfortunately, the "black panthers" used violence to achieve their goals and sadly caused the death of many people who stood in their way (Foner, 1988).

While the "black panthers" led a violent fight, we must not say that the civil rights movement was focused primarily on violence. Once again, America saw the renaissance of an extraordinary man who was Dr. Martin Luther King Jr., who fought for all men to have equal rights. He used non-violence as an emblem on August 28th 1963 at the "March on Washington" (Bayard, 1963). The march touched thousands of hearts leaving audiences in tears with his powerful words as they grasped the intense struggle he faced, causing the union of white and black Americans together for one purpose, equal rights, which included the right to vote and the right to eliminate segregation in all states of the United States. The whole media began accepting his fight and regarded him as a reputable source, displaying his words for everyone to hear and understand.

As a result of the civil rights movement, America experienced an awakening of a new beginning. Consequently, a direct descendant of the oppressed African American generation who once suffered slavery and segregation is now the leader of the richest country in the world. No one during the time of civil rights would have guessed that a son of the late martyrs is now our Commander and Chief, Barack Obama, President of the United States of America. It is evident that he gained trusted and support of his staff, colleagues, the entire public, and even foreign leaders. Given these points, we must say that America now shares the same purpose of equality for all. The Equal Rights Amendment (ERA) added in our Constitution eliminates segregation and gives the right to vote to all men of any race. Therefore, this official government document can be viewed as a perpetual, credible way to define the importance of the equal rights which honors the dream that a great man once had (Bayard, 1963).

By: Gloria Creecy, Class of 2017

REFERENCES

Philipinasscholnet. "Professional Essay Writing Help." 2015. The civil rights movement. Writing Guides & Tips. 09 March 2016.
<http://www.pilipinasschoolnet.org/a-high-quality-example-on-alternative-energy-sources.php>.

Wikipedia. "The Free Encyclopedia." 15 March 2010. Fifteenth Amendment to the United States Constitution. document. 09 March 2016.
<https://en.wikipedia.org/wiki/Fifteenth_Amendment_to_the_United_States_Constitution>.

Window, Thematic. "The Civil Rights Movement." 2015. PBS.ORG. document. 09 March 2016.
<http://www.pbs.org/johngardner/chapters/4b.html>.

THROUGH THE LENSES OF MALCOLM X

When we think about the Civil Rights Movement what comes to mind? For the most common thought there are a whole host of brave people that could be named for standing up for his or her rights or the rights of others but, the most memorable is Civil Rights Activist Dr. Martin Luther King. His major role in the Civil Rights Movement taught nonviolent activism, brought about peaceful protest and demonstrations, the Montgomery Bus Boycott, voting rights, and a call to action for love, peace, and integration. On the other end of the spectrum "the angriest Negro in America" (373), a man known to the world as Malcolm X, went about addressing his feelings of indifference towards the roles and treatment of African Americans totally opposite of Dr. King and backed a lot of his feelings and views with the religious knowledge he had received.

Malcolm X, born Malcolm Little, was born in to a family of eight children. He lived with his very educated mother Louise Little and father Reverend Earl Little who was a Baptist Minister and devoted supporter of Black Nationalist Leader Marcus Garvey in Omaha, Nebraska. Malcolm's family was poverty stricken and had to live in fear and be very cautious of white attacks which taunted their family very often, causing them to relocate many times. Malcolm recalls, "we were standing outside in our underwear, crying and yelling our heads off. The white police and fireman came and stood around watching as the house burned to the ground" (Haley 3). This was a result of one of the house fires cause by two white men and Malcolm expressed the police and fireman's little concern for his family now out of a home. From a young age Malcolm had already formulated a different distinctive mindset that set him apart from the rest that he would later act upon in his adult years. At a very young age Malcolm made up in his mind that "they were much better off than the negroes who would shout, as his father preached, for the pie-in-the-sky and the heaven hereafter while the white man had his here on earth" (Haley 6). After the brutal murder of his father which Malcolm believes was the actions of the Black Legion who harassed his family daily, Malcolm's life spiraled downhill quickly. His mother lost her way religiously becoming a Seventh-Day-Adventist and mentally as well, breaking down due to the loss of her husband. After his mother was committed into a mental hospital, he was adopted and later moved to Boston where he lived the stereotypical life a black man dealing with hardcore drugs, drinking, hustling, and stealing until it landed him ten years in prison. There is where he found the Nation of Islam through his brother and developed a lot of his central beliefs.

Elijah Muhammad, a messenger of Allah for the Nation of Islam, was Malcolm X's idol. He looked up to him and respected every aspect of his teachings. Muhammad taught that Christianity was a white man's religion and that Christianity was a way to keep black people enslaved referring to white people as "blue-eyed devils" and that they are evil by nature. After revaluating and accepting these teachings as his own, Malcolm X became one of the top minsters for the Nation of Islam spreading this same message, converting people all over especially young black men. Malcom X believed that white society worked to keep African Americans from empowering themselves and achieving political, economic, and social success. He proclaimed that he was living in a world with "a shameful case of minority oppression" (Haley 183). He felt that Black men saw themselves as only an "internal United States issue because of 'Civil Rights'" (Haley 183). He questioned "how is the black man going to get 'civil rights' before he wins his human rights?"(Haley 183). He believed that "the black man didn't have economic strength—and it would take time for him to build it but right now the American black man has the political strength and power to change his destiny overnight" (Haley 322). With this type of mindset Malcolm's views contradicted the teachings of Dr. King during the Civil Rights Movement.

Dr. King was a Christian activist that stood for nonviolence and promoted integration amongst people of all race, color, religion, and creed. Malcolm X was a firm believer of Allah but he claimed, "I believe in Christ, not Christianity" (Haley 292). They were similar because they both wanted a better more successful life for African Americans. Whereas Dr. King promoted the "turn the other cheek" philosophy Malcolm X said "Do nothing unto anyone that you would not like have done to you. Seek peace, and never be the aggressor but if anyone attacks you, we do not teach you to turn the other cheek" (Haley 218). Malcolm was accused by white people of teaching black supremacy and hate. He was called "a teacher, a fomenter of violence" (Haley 373). His response was just, "I'm not for wanton violence, I'm for justice" (Haley 373). Because of the constant setbacks of African Americans with no support of the government, he felt "if the law fails to protect Negroes from whites' attack, then those Negroes should use arms, if necessary, to defend themselves" (Haley 373). Malcolm felt as though it was time to fight back against those who oppressed blacks for so long and he felt that Dr. King just wasn't getting the job done as efficiently as it could have been done. No, violence is not the answer, but those hot tempered people that were told they could not march with Dr. King because there would be no fighting back easily gravitated to Malcolm who advocated armed Negroes and that "Negroes have the right to fight against racist, by any means that are necessary" (Haley 374). He was "for violence if non-violence meant African Americans continue to postpone a solution to the American Black man's problem just to avoid violence" (Haley 374).

Integration was the ultimate solution for Dr. King and it was also the ultimate problem for Malcolm X! Malcolm believed that blacks should just live amongst their own kind and why would African Americans want to integrate with whites after all they did to their ancestors from slavery to the constant brain washing and socially and economically beat downs present day. After all, whites didn't want anything to do with the blacks anyway so why want to be in the presence of someone who don't want you there in the first place. He said that "No sane black man really wants integration! No sane white man wants integration!" (Haley 250). Malcolm felt that African Americans should be able to step up and govern themselves businesses, economically, politically, in all aspects. He wanted an intentional separation division between whites and blacks. "We reject 'segregation' even more militantly than you say you do! We want 'separation', which is not the same! The Honorable Elijah Muhammad teaches us that 'segregation' is when your life and liberty are controlled, regulated, by someone else. To 'segregate' means to control. Segregation is that which is forced upon inferiors by superiors. But 'separation' is that which is done voluntarily, by two equals — for the good of both!" (Haley 250). While expressing his idea of a greater need for separation amongst whites and blacks it also brought a separation in belief systems because America believed Christianity and the Nation of Islam was growing. He wanted America to understand Islam because he believed "this is one religion that erases from its society the race problem. After his trip to the Holy Land, Mecca he was exposed to what so many different aspects that altered his views towards the Nation of Islam and his central beliefs. In Mecca is where he became an official Muslim and it was there that he realized and felt that the religion of Islam brought people together because he said "he talked to white people but the 'white' attitude was removed from their minds by the religion of Islam" (Haley 347). One of his discoveries in Mecca was the white Muslims, something that was very

unusual in America so that definitely shifted his perception about white people and religion and exposed the faulty teachings of the Honorable Elijah Muhammad. He believed that "the whites and blacks that he fellowshipped with was truly the same because their belief in one God have removed the white, their minds, behavior, and attitudes" (Haley 347).

Malcolm's views might have seemed unreasonable or unrealistic to some but they were very logical. First one has to examine where Malcolm came from, his background, and his family history. Malcolm grew up with violence surrounding him and racism and death knocking at his front door. He lost all his uncles and his father due to hate crimes that could have been halted by the government but they weren't because of the color of his skin. He had been oppressed financially and economically struggling all throughout his growing up years that contributed to this anger that had built up in him. Living on the streets of Boston, he watched his Black brothers' struggle and the white man never reached out a helping hand starting with the white man in the White House. These struggles in his eyes were pulling the black man down.

Given Malcolm's experiences, his strong relationship with Elijah Muhamad and the Nation of Islam gave him something to believe in and build off of. He was so into the teachings that it pushed him to learn more about the world around him; he became self-educated and even went out on explorations across the world. He believed in Brotherhood and the empowerment of the black brotherhood, and his curiosity about the true Nation of Islam exposed him to a greater picture of true brotherhood and oneness amongst all races.

By: Breana Dabney, Class of 2018

A VIOLENT CYCLE

Malcolm: Where Am I?

Socrates: Malcolm, dear thinker from the 20th century, a public orator, a Muslim: welcome to Limbo. You are not alone. Aristotle, Archimedes, Bertrand Russell, and Ludwig Wittgenstein are here as well. Come and relax: this is eternity for you now.

Malcolm: Never could I… I never committed an injustice: the laws on Earth committed the injustice to me. I don't deserve this…

Socrates: What is justice though, Malcolm? For if you never committed it, surely you should be able to define it and tell me of its meaning.

Malcolm: Justice is at the core of all basic human interaction. It defines the laws that that we use to interact with each other, which in turn controls our behaviors with the constant goal in mind to better our overall wellbeing. Injustice, Socrates, is when this justice spoken about in the later isn't happening. It is when one group or person is excluded from this idea of improving the status quo and is treated as an outcast. My African American people are outside of this law in the United States. We are the outcasts in a white-minded society.

Socrates: Malcolm, when you say outcasts, do you imply that theses outcasts must take a certain route of action? Or should they accept the injustice at hand?

Malcolm: I mean to say that you can not be neutral: you can not heed to laws that exclude your very input on their creation in the first place. It is not just, Socrates. It is a sort of cultural imprisonment. One in which I intend to break out of.

Socrates: And how do you intend to break out of this imprisonment?

Malcolm: There are two ways of doing this. Both are justified off of this idea of exclusion from justice. And when any group experiences the later, it is their duty to refute the injustice. Start off by demanding a say in the law once more. If that fails, then I say, when the laws do not represent that one person or group, they may act outside of those laws imposed on them. Violence has just been justified and must be used to expose the injustice at hand.

Socrates: Do you mean to say that violence can make an injustice noticeable?

Malcolm: Yes, I do.

Socrates: And by making it noticeable, violence can therefore bring about a proper solution to the problem? Possibly ending the injustice?

Malcolm: I mean to say that violence can escalate a smaller conflict into a larger dilemma. Nothing short of what my African American people need: global recognition. Because Socrates, they are fighting for basic human rights. By putting the issue on a global scale, the injustice becomes recognizable as a human rights conflict. All of this points out that what is called a civil rights struggle is actually a human rights struggle, which comes from natural rights given to us all from birth.

Socrates: I see. And so this path of violence makes justice the ultimate authority once more?

Malcolm: Yes, it does.

Socrates: When you say this, do you mean to say that justice does not have a higher authority?

Malcolm: Yes.

Socrates: I see. Let us look at the arguments you gave and break it down piece by piece. Maybe then we can prove the argument in your favor, or, maybe we can find the flaws in the logic and build upon them. Does this sound plausible for you?

Malcolm: Socrates, I see no further argument.

Socrates: I only wish to prove what you call justice in front of you. Surely if your argument are as concise as you say, then the argument must be true, is it not?

Malcolm: It is indeed.

Socrates: Then please walk me through your logic as I trail behind its path to better understand its steps. For when you say justice has no higher authority, do you mean to say that justice has nothing else to report to?

Malcolm: I do not understand.

Socrates: Let me reiterate. Is justice not a truth?

Malcolm: It is indeed a truth.

Socrates: So justice is therefore a truth?

Malcolm: Undoubtedly.

Socrates: And If it is a truth, it falls under the many other truths, such as a square having four sides and two plus two equaling four, all of which are the truths that all humans rationally know upon birth?

Malcolm: Yes, you can say that.

Socrates: It seems that justice therefore does have a higher authority of Truth. Something that must always be heeded to if justice is to not become an injustice, correct?

Malcolm: ...yes, yes indeed.

Socrates: Let us stay in line with this logic of calling Truth the higher order that guides our reasoning and decisions, and lets walk through your argument step by step.

Malcolm: So be it.

Socrates: Malcolm, is physical harm to another an evil deed?

Malcolm: It can be, depending on the circumstances.

Socrates: Let us take another approach: for when I say harm, I mean that physical harm can damage a person's character that is the foundation to who they are. This is the type of harm that can ruin a person's character and grounding. In this sense, is harm an evil deed?

Malcolm: Yes, yes it is.

Socrates: So harm is an evil deed because of this?

Malcolm: Yes.

Socrates: And harm is therefore contrary to good?

Malcolm: Yes.

Socrates: And it can lead to actual harm, which damages another person's character, the foundation of who they are?

Malcolm: Yes.

Socrates: But it can lead to harm. Thus the consequences are not always intentional or expected, correct?

Malcolm: Yes, the results cannot always be known.

Socrates: Malcolm, is violence a form of harm to others?

Malcolm: Yes, in my case it is deliberately so.

Socrates: And can it do harm to another human because of this?

Malcolm: Yes, it runs the possibility of doing do.

Socrates: Malcolm, is good not superior to evil?

Malcolm: It is indeed so.

Socrates: Is this therefore part of the family of Truths we spoke about previously?

Malcolm: It is indeed so…

Socrates: And if violence is therefore evil, is it not contrary to good?

Malcolm: Yes, it is contrary to good…

Socrates: And therefore, is violence not in line with the family of universal Truths that we spoke about previously?

Malcolm: It is not in line…

Socrates: Violence must therefore never be justified despite the circumstances: for doing harm to another human being is evil and is therefore contrary to the universal Truths, which is the authority to justice. Your cultural group, the outcasts, must therefore resist the violent path in search for another. For if there is an injustice, it should not be accepted as you stated earlier, correct?

Malcolm: This is true.

Socrates: And this is because the basic rights of justice are meant for all, and not a sub group of the whole group, correct?

Malcolm: Yes, correct.

Socrates: And the first step is an attempt at dialogue, as you said previously, correct?

Malcolm: Yes, of course.

Socrates: Shortly after you mentioned breaking the law if the law does not work in your favor, in this case, if the law does not properly represent you, correct?

Malcolm: This is correct.

Socrates: But Malcolm, is law not a social agreement of some sorts?

Malcolm: I do not understand.

Socrates: Let me explain. When a law is put into place, regardless of who decrees it, it is bestowed upon an entire people. After, the polity is told to accept these laws. Isn't this very acceptance a sort of social contract of sorts? One in which all parties must at least recognize the law?

Malcolm: I see. Recognize yes, but heed to, no.

Socrates: Yes, but at least recognize, correct?

Malcolm: Yes, I agree.

Socrates: Malcolm, is committing to violence not acting directly contrary to the laws. For the laws declare what crimes are to be called violent, correct?

Malcolm: Yes, the law tells us what sorts of actions are violent.

Socrates: But don't all who live under the law that calls an action violent recognize the laws that declare such an action to be so?

Malcolm: Yes... this is true.

Socrates: Malcolm, is not the very act of violence an act of criticism to the laws, which is a template for the behavior that the polity expects?

Malcolm: Yes...

Socrates: Therefore, the act of violence is a direct action taken against the law, which harms the social contract that the group or person has committed to along with his fellow humans within the polity. Malcolm, I can not help but say that because violence is evil, that perhaps substituting your philosophy of violence for good and virtuous actions in favor of a political voice for all would fair better than harming others and hoping to have your voice heard. Malcolm, know that this is not a direct criticism, but the corollaries of our arguments.

Malcolm: I see, Socrates...

Socrates: Come Malcolm, let us continue to argue, for eternity will pass us by here in the grand inferno. Here, we can seek justice in its purest form through the lessons that we teach each other through skillful argumentation and diligent listening to each other.

Malcolm: Let us.

By: Daniel Gomez, Class of 2019

Note: The assignment which elicited this response can be found in the Teaching Notes which appear at the conclusion of the Anthology.

IN LIVING COLOR: BOSTON BUSING

Boston, a bustling city not unlike Philadelphia with vibrant history and colonial background. In a time of hot fury of the Civil Rights movement, the Boston segregation of busing was a dark and often forgotten moment in our nation's Civil Rights history. When we think of this period in America we think down south. We think of bus boycotts when Americans refused to go on the bus. Often however we forget the moments when Americans were forced to go on the bus. When the Civil Rights moment is remembered it often brings images of the south, sweltering Alabama sit-ins and Martin Luther King Jr's rich drawl preaching to a horde of millions. Less remembered perhaps is the turmoil as Boston schools were forced to desegregate and the backlash that occurred as educational history was formed in the ashes.

Voices in Boston shot out, claiming more than dissatisfaction but a crime being committed. There were no Bostonian black principals and hardly one teacher was black out of 200 by the year 1965. In that same year, the legislature of Massachusetts resounded with the Racial Imbalance Act. This act required schools "with more than 50 percent of students of one race to desegregate," or possibly lose funding (Gellerman, 2014). This took schools that had almost 100 percent whites in South Boston and the schools that were predominantly black in Roxbury to switch. This was met with fierce opposition mainly from whites of the working class.

In 1974 the United States District court of Massachusetts mandated that all public school of Boston must be desegregated. To do this students were plucked from their schools and the communities they knew and their parents knew and were forced to take transportation to a completely new school system. Blacks would go to white schools and vice versa.

The outcome of this implementation ultimately led to an extreme decline in attendance and eventually development in suburban living.

To say the desegregation of Boston buses was successful is like saying the Doolittle Raid on Japan was successful. In theory perhaps, but at what cost? Parents watched their children board the buses headed for the opposite side of the city, some an hour each way and wondered what right the government had to dictate schooling. (Irons, Murphy, Russell, n.d)

Like all cities, Boston relied greatly on busing to get citizens, especially students, from place to place. Although the overall objective of desegregation was noble, at a time of racial tension the coercive forcing that was sought out was seen as unlawful by many.

In order to give students the best possible means of success and fed up with the lack of resources, black parents boycotted schools and put their children in "separate Freedom Schools," which were hosted by the committee.

These school committees that had been indecently elected rebutted that the segregated schools were the product of social condition and thus, "beyond their control" (PBS).

It was then in summer of 1974 that the Massachusetts Judge Arthur W. Garrity took the case and declared in Morgan v. Hannagan they were going to "take the two racially separate schools committee and intertwine them." Looking at 1954's Brown V. The Board of Education he made blacks and whites attend each other's schools (Gellerman).

Almost immediately there was backlash, and before a single student had stepped through the door of the opposite school there were not only pickets and protests but rallies at the Boston Government Center and Boston City Hall. This was to be only the beginning. On the first day of school in in September of 1974, enormous, violent crowds gathered, held back only by police. Stone, bottles and horrific slurs were jeered and hurled at the arriving black students by awaiting white crowds. Buses were damaged, hundreds of state troops and the Massachusetts National Guard were called in. Chaos that we have long associated with the turbulent Civil Rights era in the south was in full swing that day in the north.

The statistics couldn't cover up the failure of the attempt. "Of 1,300 black Roxbury students assigned to South Boston, only 100 showed up that day." In the predominantly black neighborhood of Roxbury, just 13 white students went to school by order's initial day (Gellerman).

Eventually, eventually, order was moderately established and a gradual attendance was set. However enough black families refused to participate completely that communities established "Freedom schools," hosted by the community. There was soon an influx of whites to the suburbs. Those who would rather move completely to private schools than comply with the public schooling order. Nowadays Boston is desegregated like the rest of America but memories of the events linger through prejudices today.

Nowadays many of us think very little about sharing a classroom with a member of a different race and those who use a different dialog when speaking or share a different religion than us. At La Salle University we are taught the importance of service and the necessity of togetherness. We are encouraged to connect with those different than us and come together as we find out what it means to be "Explorers."

Now more than forty years later, the Boston desegregation movement is still affecting city schools as schools still face enrollment problems although the lines of segregations are more blurred and schools are more accessible to student's regardless of race. Still, a fateful turn of events unfolded not too long ago, witnessed by our parents and grandparents. If America is to be the great melting pot we proclaim it to be, we must always remember the past and learn from it. The tagline from the movement to desegregate Boston schools was, "For truth, learning, and change," and that can still be applied today (Handy, 2012).

Segregation wasn't just tolerated in the south, all over the country Civil Rights advancement laws were fought and progress was slow. Desegregation is still a modern process we deal with all over the country and the world. Despite what hasn't made the history books, it's still relevant. The Civil Rights Era is hardly over. Today we still have protests over inequality and fights against racial division. As Americans citizens we must learn from every instance and always strive to do better than previous years.

By Andrea Grabenstein, Class of 2016

REFERENCES

Boston Desegregation. (n.d.). Retrieved May 07, 2016, from http://www.pbslearningmedia.org/resource/iml04.soc.ush.civil.boston/boston-desegregation/

Gellerman, B. (2014, December 19). How The Boston Busing Decision Still Affects City Schools 40 Years Later. Retrieved May 06, 2016, from http://www.wbur.org/2014/06/20/boston-busing-ruling-anniversary

Handy, D. (2012, March 30). 40 Years Later, Boston Looks Back On Busing Crisis. Retrieved May 11, 2016, from http://www.wbur.org/2012/03/30/boston-busing-crisis

Irons, M. E., Murphy, S., & Russell, J. (n.d.). History rolled in on a yellow school bus - The Boston Globe. Retrieved May 10, 2016, from https://www.bostonglobe.com/metro/2014/09/06/boston-busing-crisis-years-later/DS35nsuqp0yh8f1q9aRQUL/story.html

AFFIRMATIVE ACTION

The United States of America is a country that is inhabited by a large number of people in love with capitalism. The concept of capitalism involves having businesses privately owned, rather than the government owning business entities. A true capitalist would argue that the government should be completely laissez faire when it comes to economics, however this is not a reasonable economic plan. Unregulated corporate greed would incubate and run rampant throughout society and the "little guy," or the "minority" groups, would be crushed. There is nothing wrong with capitalism, but it is still the duty of government to impose laws that make a fair playing field for all parties involved. One category of the law that immediately comes to mind that combats the free will of corporations and the oppression of underrepresented minorities in the business world is affirmative action.

There are several different opinions on affirmative action, but in order to have an educated opinion on it, one must become informed. "Employers often adopt affirmative action plans, which provide that certain job preference will be given to members of minority racial and ethnic groups, females, and other protected-class applicants, when an employer makes an employment decision" (Cheeseman 558). However, affirmative action policies that have been put into place by corporations and other entities may not exist if it was not for the federal statute of Title VII of the Civil Rights Act of 1964. The act states, "it shall be an unlawful employment practice for an employer ... to discriminate against any individual with respect to his compensation, terms, conditions, or privileges of employment, because of such individual's race, color, religion, sex, or national origin" (Know Your Rights). This federal statute's aim was to eliminate discrimination because many people, especially minorities, were being discriminated against in the workplace. Fairness was the key idea that drove the indoctrination of Title VII.

Title VII of the Civil Rights Act of 1964 provided the necessary groundwork for affirmative action policies to be put into place. "Title VII of the Civil Rights Act of 1964 outlawed discrimination in employment based on race, color, national origin, sex, and religion. The law clearly prohibited any further discrimination based upon these protected classes. However, did the federal statute intend to grant a favorable status to the classes of persona who had previously been discriminated against?" (Cheeseman 523). This excerpt kicks off the discussion of affirmative action by Cheeseman. The book continues on saying, "In a series of cases, the U.S. Supreme Court upheld the use of affirmative action programs to make up for egregious past discrimination, particularly based on race" (Cheeseman 523).

One particular landmark affirmative action case is "Regents of the University of California v. Bakke." It was a case that dealt with Bakke, a white man, suing for reverse discrimination in regards to his admittance into a university.

One of the true landmark cases in Supreme Court history, the Bakke decision found a way to uphold some parts of affirmative action while rejecting other parts. Allan Bakke, a white man, had twice applied for admission to the University of California Medical School at Davis. He was rejected both times, despite having the required academic achievements, while minority applicants were given preference. The court decided the University of California had to admit Bakke, arguing the rigid use of racial quotas at the school violated the Equal Protection Clause of the 14th Amendment. But the court also found that race as part of admissions decisions was constitutional, as long as it was one of several admission criteria (yahoo).

This case sparks particular interest because it involves the college admission process, which many people go through in their life. This case sets that precedent that shapes affirmative action policies. Universities, companies and any other entity that require "admission" cannot reserve seats for certain minority groups. Many people in the majority, such as Bakke have argued that affirmative action is reverse discrimination. However, as the case states, and the textbook more explicitly states, "the courts have held that if an affirmative action plan is based on pre-established numbers or percentage quotas for hiring or promoting minority applicants, then it causes illegal reverse discrimination" (Cheeseman 523). California v. Bakke also sets forth the argument that affirmative action is the antithesis of merit hiring. Bakke ended up being granted admission to the school and the ruling was that a quota-based affirmative action policy is illegal.

Confusion about affirmative action policies arise out of people thinking that affirmative action is actually a law. Affirmative action is not actually a law, rather policies supported by case law and legislative made law. As we have discussed in class, our court system has been used numerous times to make rulings on laws. Laws such as Title VII can be vague, and for some parties, affirmative action plans developed in light of Title VII can be seen as unfair. However, the courts have clearly stated what they expect out of affirmative action plans.

After studying the Bakke case one realizes that rather than having a quota, companies need to find a way to legally and ethically develop an affirmative action plan. "To be lawful, an affirmative action plan must be narrowly tailored to achieve some compelling interest" (Cheeseman 558). It is important to understand that before looking to develop an affirmative action policy for one's own company. One interesting aspect of how affirmative action policies develop is through an order by the courts. "Plans can be voluntarily adopted by employers, undertaken to settle a discrimination action, or ordered by the courts" (Cheeseman 523). Besides the voluntary development of a plan by the employer, the courts can step in and mandate that a plan gets enacted. This is a rare result compared to an employer enacting an affirmative action on his or her own, but still interesting.

One aspect of affirmative action that people get confused about, besides accusing it of being "reverse discrimination," is comparing it to "equal opportunity employment." Many employers do not need to have affirmative action plans, but almost every employer is required to be an equal opportunity employer. "This means that even though they are not required to actively seek out minority employees, companies are also not allowed to discriminate against minorities in their hiring, firing, or workplace policies. This means that company cannot refuse to hire and cannot fire someone based on their race" (Small Business). This seems very similar to what affirmative action is, but it is actually starkly different because affirmative action plans have the active pursuit aspect, but equal opportunity employers are only required not to discriminate. There is a fine line, which is why it is easy to understand why people get mixed up between the two.

Therefore, in order to further understand what affirmative action is, it is important to review what it is not. Affirmative action is not reverse discrimination. Affirmative action plans are not meant to be policies that take away opportunities from the majority (white males). Affirmative action policies are important because they find talent for the company that would not have otherwise been considered based on the way they look. Affirmative action policies make diversity just one major factor of the long list of criteria for hiring candidates. After studying affirmative action in depth, one can never say "they were hired because they were black." The diverse candidates are just as talented as the other candidates in the applicant pool and one can assume these diverse candidates would get hired without the policies. However, history shows this is not the case and that in order to ensure that corporations get staffed with people from all walks of life, affirmative action policies are put into place. This is the 21st century and the United States is still a thriving cultural melting pot. In order for "We the People" to achieve full prosperity everyone needs to be granted their fair shot at the American Dream.

Thanks to the statutes and cases that have contributed to the development of a consistent view on "Title VII of the Civil Rights Act of 1964" there have been several great affirmative action policies enacted across the country. The difference between equal opportunity and affirmative action in the workplace has been made clearer. Most importantly, it is understood why, despite our heavily capitalistic business environment where free will to hire and fire as you please is viewed as valuable, affirmative action policies still take hold in our business environment. Before studying in-depth the concept of affirmative action, I was skeptical because like many others, I felt as though it was reverse discrimination for someone like me. After studying what affirmative action truly means, I understand why those policies are so important. Affirmative action policies are not only great for the minorities they assist, but they also enhance the overall environment of our business world. Diversity is great for businesses and in such a team based, fast-paced business environment, it is important to have a workforce that is made up of people from all walks of life.

By: Michael Ryan, Class of 2017

REFERENCES

"Are Employers Required to Have Affirmative Action Plans - FindLaw." Findlaw. N.p., n.d. Web. 07 Oct. 2015.

Cheeseman, Henry R. "Ethics and Social Responsibility of Business." Business Law. 8th ed. Upper Saddle River: Pearson Learning Solutions, 2013. 710-723. Print.

"Know Your Rights: Title VII of the Civil Rights Act of 1964." AAUW Empowering Women Since 1881 Know Your Rights Title VII of the Civil Rights Act of 1964 Comments. N.p., n.d. Web. 07 Oct. 2015.

Regents of Univ. of California v. Bakke 438 U.S. 265 (1978)

Staff, NCC. Yahoo! News. Yahoo!, n.d. Web. 07 Oct. 2015.

IN LIVING COLOR: AN ANTHOLOGY
DIVERSITY

Our Fourth Amendment states, "Shall any State deprive any person of life, liberty or property, without due process of law; nor deny to any person within its jurisdiction the equal protection of the law." These are powerful words that were adopted in 1792 however throughout the course of history the Fourth Amendment was tested many times. After reading Chapter 4 of Halbert and Ingulli, I began to realize how far we have come as a country.[1] When reading through the court cases, especially some of the older ones, I was shocked that someone would even need to have to go to trial over a clear violation of the mean of "Equality for all." Even though it shocked me, it also reflects just how we as a country have moved forward. Our country is becoming more diverse every day and so is our workforce. However, how has diversity affected businesses in general?

Research shows that companies with diverse leadership perform better, on both equity returns and earnings margins, than their non-diverse counterparts. A 2012 McKinsey report shows for companies ranking in the top quartile of executive-board diversity, Revenues over expenses ("ROEs") were 53 percent higher, on average, than they were for those in the bottom quartile. At the same time, EBIT (earnings before interest, taxes depreciation and amortization) margins at the most diverse companies were 14 percent high, on average, than those of the least diverse companies. This statistic alone shows the pure power that diversity brings. Many companies now have designated diversity as a strategic goal and started building it into the guts of the organization.[2]

Of all the diversity changes I believe women in the workplace have been the strongest ingredient to the success that diversity brings. A McKinsey & Company study found that the increase in women's overall share of labor in the United States went from holding 37 percent of all jobs to 47 percent over the past 40 years; this has accounted for about a quarter of current GDP.[2] Business need to realize our country is changing fast and if they do not learn to accept diversity and all the benefits it brings, they will not succeed in the future. The most recent Census data concludes that by 2050 there will be no racial or ethnic majority in our country. Also between 2000 and 2050 new

---

[1] Halbert, Terri and Elaine Ingulli, Law & Ethics in the Business Environment (2012).
[2] Barta, Thomas, Markus Kleiner, and Tilo Neumann. "Insights & Publications. "Is There a Payoff from Top-team Diversity? McKinsey & Company, Apr. 2012 Web. 20 Sept. 2013.
http://www.mckinsey.com/insights/organization/is_there_apayoff_from_top-team_diversity.

immigrants and their children will account for 83 percent of the growth in the working-age populations.[3]

Like every president has said, small businesses and entrepreneurs are the backbone of our country. Well our nation's entrepreneurs are becoming more diverse than ever before. According to the Census Bureau, people of color own 22.1 percent of U.S. businesses. Moreover, women own 28.8 percent of U.S. Businesses, and Latina-owned businesses in particular are the fastest-growing segment of the women-owned business market. According to the National Gay and Lesbian Chamber of Commerce, gay or transgender individuals own approximately 1.4 million, or approximately 5 percent of U.S. businesses.[4] This fact shows entrepreneurs plus diversity is truly the backbone of our nation and what makes America so great.

Of all the diversity changes I believe women in the workplace have been the strongest ingredient to the success that diversity brings. A McKinsey & Company study found that the increase in women's overall share of labor in the United States went from holding 37 percent of all jobs to 47 percent over the past 40 years; this has accounted for about a quarter of current GDP.[2] Business need to realize our country is changing fast and if they do not learn to accept diversity and all the benefits it brings, they will not succeed in the future. The most recent Census data concludes that by 2050 there will be no racial or ethnic majority in our country. Also between 2000 and 2050 new immigrants and their children will account for 83 percent of the growth in the working-age populations.[5]

Like every president has said, small businesses and entrepreneurs are the backbone of our country. Well our nation's entrepreneurs are becoming more diverse than ever before. According to the Census Bureau, people of color own 22.1 percent of U.S. businesses. Moreover, women own 28.8 percent of U.S. Businesses, and Latina-owned businesses in particular are the fastest-growing segment of the women-owned business market. According to the National Gay and Lesbian Chamber of Commerce, gay or transgender individuals own approximately 1.4 million, or approximately 5 percent of U.S.

---

[3] Kerby, Sophia, and Crosby Burns. "The Top 10 Economic Facts of Diversity in the Workplace." Center for American Progress. N.p., July 2012. Web 20 Sept. 2013. Http://www.americanprogress.org/issues/labor/news/2012/07/12/11900/the-top-10-economic-facts-of-diversity-in-the-workplace/.

[4] Klein, Karen E. "How 'Diversity Fatigue' Undermines Business Growth." BloombergBusinessWeek. N.P., 14 May 2012. Web. 20 Sept. 2013. http://www.businessweek.com/articles/2012-05-14/how-diversity-fatigue-undermines-business-growth.

[5] Kerby and Burns

businesses.[6] This fact shows entrepreneurs plus diversity is truly the backbone of our nation and what makes America so great.

A diverse workforce combines workers from different backgrounds and experiences that together breed a more creative, innovative, and productive workforce. Businesses have learned that they can draw upon our nation's diversity to strengthen their bottom line. Diversity is a key ingredient to growing a strong and economy that's built to last.

By Scott Barist, MBA 2014

---

[6] Klein

BLACK LIVES MATTER!

Black lives matter!

They always have and they always will. However lives don't seem to matter in New York, who constantly reminds us that they are the so called "Greatest City in the World," when the breath of a man can be taken away, for peddling cigarettes, until it results in his ultimate death.

Apparently, lives do not matter in Ferguson, Missouri where no dignity was shown for the body of a young man left uncovered in the street, after he was gunned down and killed by a police officer in broad daylight.

Who among us can convince the residents of Cleveland, Ohio that lives matter, regardless of age, when one of the city's "Finest," charged with protecting those same residents, can shoot and kill a child in a playground? A place which should be a safe haven for all children not a "Killing Field."

Today, we find ourselves at the very least in a precarious situation that if not properly and timely addressed, will result in dire consequences for all of us, not just in this country but throughout the entire world.

To say that the world has become smaller is not just a popular trivial saying. It truly has. When breaking news occurs on continents far away they can be reported on and made known to the world in minutes and videos of incidents occurring anywhere on the globe can go viral almost instantaneously, then the world has truly "become smaller." When the previously mentioned and similar events occur here and throughout the world, we are soon made aware of them, and no matter your opinion is as to what led up to the event, a life that mattered to someone has taken away.

However, in this precarious situation we are presently in there is also an opportunity for each and every one of us. An opportunity to make a difference, to offer your talents, to contribute your time, in making this a world where fairness, respect, and justice is applied to all of us. Each of you are capable of more than you realize, and if a drop of rain becomes current in the ocean, how much more powerful are you and all that you have to offer to the world in affecting change. Let us be inspired by Margaret Mead, the anthropologist who reminded us to "Never believe that a few caring people can't change the world. For, indeed, that's all who ever have."

In his 1963 speech the Reverend Martin Luther King stated, "The ultimate measure of a man is not where he stands in moments of comfort and convenience, but where he stands at times of challenge and controversy. The true neighbor will risk his position, his prestige, and even his life for the welfare of others. In dangerous valleys and hazardous pathways, he will lift some bruised and beaten brother to a higher and more noble life." As Lasallians we are imbued with a Spirit of unyielding Faith that allows us to step out of our comfort zones, put aside conveniences, and use our talents to take on challenges and controversy that will in effect change in the world.

From the foundation of this great university we have been afforded a platform to make a change by being a voice for the voiceless, a vote for the disenfranchised, and models for inspiring the uninspired. Your voice matters and it is your charge to use it unflinchingly to make a change that will create a world, an environment, a place where all "Lives Matter."

By: Ayanna Fuller, Class of 2015

UNTITLED

"The oldest and strongest emotion of mankind is fear, and the oldest and strongest kind of fear is fear of the unknown"

– H. P. Lovecraft, Supernatural Horror in Literature

In my last reading response I wrote concerning that most impressive value of our Founders, equality. As I stated the Founders sought to build a society wherein everyone would be equal, and free to pursue their own happiness. However, I also referred to our actions as their philosophical successors, and arrived at the conclusion that we had failed them in the goal they set for us. While we have moved towards equality through court rulings and the acts of legislation, we still have not overcome the basis on which modern day inequality is founded, fear.

While the above quote from H.P. Lovecraft does not directly refer to fear leading to discrimination, it does sum up the tendency of man to fear that which is different from him. Throughout the history of humanity we, as a species, have sought for ways to subdivide ourselves. Gender, color, faith, and sexuality have all become personal identifiers that we have used to single ourselves out from the population as a whole. We seek the company of others like ourselves because we feel more connected to them, and we ostracize and drive out those who are not because we fear their difference.

Perhaps, deep down, we are just seeking to preserve our own uniqueness. We all, at one time or another, have felt the desire to be recognized as special. Each one of us seeks that one thing at which we are the best, and we are driven to pursue that one thing our entire lives. If we allowed people of different colors or faiths to mix with us, then we might realize that we aren't particularly special. We might see that others can do the same things that we can, and might even be able to do them better. This in turn would force us to realize our own shortcomings.

As society has grown more heterogeneous, different peoples have been thrust together, oftentimes against their will. This trend has met with resistance in the form of hatred and discrimination. Dominant groups seeks to preserve their dominance thought legislation and force, fearing that if they do not they will be overrun and subjugated themselves. It is this fear which has led to such horrible institutions as slavery, apartheid, and even concentration camps.

Yes there is hope that through exposure and learning, this fear can be overcome. We have seen examples in our own country that give credence to this hope. Slavery was abolished, women were given the same rights as men, and more recently homosexual couples won several legal battles to obtain their right to marry. In each of these cases society came to realize that the groups seeking rights were not looking to seize power, but only to obtain that very equality which our Founders sought themselves.

By Robert C. Ristow, MBA 2014

A TRUE NEIGHBOR

"The ultimate measure of a man is not where he stands in moments of comfort and convenience, but where he stands at times of challenge and controversy. The true neighbor will risk his position, his prestige, and even his life for the welfare of others. In dangerous valleys and hazardous pathways, he will lift some bruised and beaten brother to a higher and more noble life."

– Martin Luther King, Jr., Strength to Love, 1963

Martin Luther King Jr. was an outstanding man. He dedicated his life to making sure people treated each other with dignity, love and respect. Martin Luther King Jr. died in his efforts to ensure justice for all. Currently we are still fighting a similar racial battle in the United States of America. Racial tensions peaked with the recent grand jury decisions in Ferguson and New York. We must decide where we want to go from here as a nation. We must decide, as individuals, what kind of people we are, and what kind of country to we want to live in and leave behind for the next generation of Americans.

I understand that there are many people who are filled with hate, anger and the desire for revenge after the recent racial incidents that have occurred. As a nation, we can move in that di-rection- with more polarization and distance between each other- or we can act the way Martin Luther King Jr. would want us to act- with compassion and understanding towards one another, to take the hatred and turn it into love.

The racial injustices that take place in our country are wrong. In order to go beyond these difficult times in our nation, we must take the time to understand. To understand how difficult it must feel to fall victim to racial injustices.

On April 4th, 1968, Dr. King was assassinated. Race riots in every major city followed in shockwaves as people heard this horrid news. Then senator of New York, Robert Kennedy, was in Indianapolis, Indiana and wanted to tell the people what had happened. The local police warned Kennedy that they would not be able to protect him if riots were to break out. Kennedy's own advisors tried to persuade him to not speak, yet he persisted on giving a speech. Kennedy stood on the back of a flatbed truck and gave one of the best speeches in U.S history. In the speech, he quotes the great poet Aeschylus. The poem states,

> "Even in our sleep, pain which cannot forget
> falls drop by drop upon the heart,
> until, in our own despair,

against our will,
comes wisdom
through the awful grace of God."

Although all major cities had riots after the news of Dr. King's death, the city of Indianapolis remained calm after Kennedy's speech. Sixty-three days after his historic speech, Kennedy was assassinated. I believed the late Robert Kennedy acted the way Dr. King would have wanted us to act when challenged by moments of controversy and uncertainty. Kennedy risked his position, his prestige, and even his life, for the welfare of others. In dangerous valleys and hazardous pathways, he stood tall and acted on what he thought was right and just. Kennedy acted as a true neighbor.

What we need in this great country of ours is the wisdom to see past racial bias, to have the courage to show compassion and love, and the intuition to act with justice.

Our great nation has had to endure difficult times before and will have to endure them in the future. We can continue to grow as a nation by seeking justice for all human beings. Let us, as the American people, dedicate ourselves to the messages Dr. King spoke of and evoke them in our everyday lives.

As the great Dr. King once said,

"Our lives begin to end the day we become silent about things that matter."

Let us devote ourselves to a higher and more noble life. Thank you and God Bless.

By: Thomas MacLeod, Class of 2015

STEPPING STONES

A shoulder to lean on.

A hand for those in need.

A sincere smile and a heartfelt hello.

Everyday is a new beginning, but to others … to others it means so much more.

"If I cannot do great things, I can do small things in a great way."

Today.

Today people are scared.

Today people are anxious.

Today people are praying.

"If I cannot do great things, I can do small things in a great way."

I cannot change the minds of those who refuse to see eye to eye.

I cannot guarantee a safe haven to all refugees.

I cannot guarantee that there will no longer be hate, but…

But I can do small things in a great way;

I will choose to keep fighting.

I will choose love over hate.

I will continue to have faith.

And I will…

"I will do small things in a great way."

Peaceful marches for a greater cause

Erasing Swastikas on the sub with hand sanitizer

Protesting at the Standing Rock Indian Reservation

Do small things in a great way."

To others, it means hope that their loved ones will be safe.

To others, it means finally being able to be treated as equals.

To others, it means hope that times will pass and we will see humanity come together again.

Every small thing we do are the stepping stones that greater good.

If I cannot do great things

If you cannot do great things

If we cannot do great things

Then we will do small things in a great way.

A shoulder to lean on.

A hand for those in need.

A sincere smile and a heartfelt hello.

By: Deysi Gonzalez Moreno, Class of 2019

QUESTIONS

UNIT 7: Hope: Finding the Inspiration, the Tools to Fight On

1. In "A True Neighbor" McLeod recalls the words of Dr. King: "Our lives begin to end the day we become silent about things that matter." Recall a time in your life when you remained silent and wished you had spoken out. Why were you silent? What inspiration might you call on or tool you might use to be inspired to speak in future

2. "In Stepping Stones," Gonzalez encourages using the tradition of Dr. King to "do small things in a great way." What small thing might you do to advance social justice and racial harmony?

3. Ryan discusses Affirmative Action policy as a government policy which has sought to even the playing field for women and minorities who have been excluded from workplace opportunities. Is there a continuing need for Affirmative Action policies? Why or why not?

4. The US Congress is and has largely been comprised of Caucasian males. Why might such a group legislate policies such as Affirmative Action and laws such as the Civil Rights Act of 1964 which disadvantages them? Is there a time when you advocated for something or someone against interest? Why?

5. Ristow uses this quotation from Lovecraft, "The oldest and strongest emotion of mankind is fear, and the oldest and strongest kind of fear is fear of the unknown." What about our world has you afraid? How will you fight against that fear? What gives you hope that you might conquer it?

TEACHING NOTES

It is our hope that the Anthology will serve as a meaningful vehicle for teaching and deep learning in the college or secondary school classroom. While there are many ways we envision it being used (and we ask our readers to share those with us) we offer some suggestions for how it can be used in a variety of ways across disciplines:

Faculty Frames: Discuss each faculty frame individually. What are the implications for research, policy, practice or wisdom shared? Have students identify an opinion or viewpoint they might reconsider based on the frame presented.

Assign or ask students to choose a faculty frame. Then assign some reading from the Anthology. Ask students to make connections between the ideas expressed in the frame and the student pieces.

False Facts? In contemporary society, perhaps now more than ever, it is important to be vigilant for opinion and misrepresentation to be parading as fact. As discussed in "A Note on Editing," we have *not* fact-checked the representations found in the student writing presented here. Have your students do so. Have them write about how they verified or disproved the representations. In years of moderating conversations on race, we observe that many student viewpoints are based on "false facts" or unsupportable assumptions, largely based on a lack of experience and education.

Citation Form Comparison: Intentionally, we have not employed a uniform system of citation in this volume. The writing was produced in different classrooms (or for competition only) and across disciplines. Some of the citation forms employed are discipline specific and others follow no standard form at all. Ask your students to identify the various forms used as APA, MLA, Bluebook, Chicago, etc. or that no standard form is employed. Have them look for a reference and experience how easy or difficult it is to find with the information given. Discuss how and why citation form and uniformity is important for the reader and in the publication of academic research.

Brave Space/Safe Space: When sharing about the Anthology contents, consider what kind of space is needed for discussion. In "brave" spaces, students share anticipating that their views will be challenged and that they will need to defend and/or reconsider preconceived notions. In "safe" spaces, students share without an expectation of confrontation, but to express concern, fear, anxiety, lack of hope and we encourage a gentle response that acknowledges their thoughts, feelings, etc. with the possibility of directing the student to resources (further reading, counselling services, legal services) that may be appropriate given what is shared. For more about facilitating dialogue, including the concepts and incorporation of brave and safe spaces, you might wish to read the chapter written by Brian Arao and Kristi Clemens found in *The Art of Effective Facilitation* (2013), Stylus Publishing, LLC. It can be found using the following link.

https://ssw.umich.edu/sites/default/files/documents/events/colc/from-safe-spaces-to-brave-spaces.pdf

Interviews: Ask students to conduct an interview of someone about issues of race and diversity. For guidance on how to structure such an exercise, see "Using the Qualitative Interview in the Classroom to Help Students Make Connections among Course Content, Social Capital, and Careers" Management Teaching Review- Inaugural Issue Vol. 1: 26-33 (2016). Have students write about and share the results of their interviews. Facilitate discussion around the results. Do patterns emerge? How are the experiences, thoughts, and feeling the same or different as those expressed in the Anthology? Consider the demographics of the persons interviewed in connection therewith. Ask students to think about how "big" or "small" or "diverse" the world is in which they live day to day. Query them on how and why they arrived at that conclusion and how living in "their world" might shape their views.

Artistic Interpretation and Creation: It is said that a picture is worth a thousand words. Student artworks appear at the end of Unit 3 and the beginning of Unit 4. Have students describe those pictures and discuss what they believe the artist is intending to portray. Have students respond to the art work with an original visual or musical creation of their own.

Go Wide and Deep Gallery: Use the student work (or excerpts therefrom) to create a Van Buskirk-London Gallery Experience referred to in the Foreword and detailed in the Reardon Faculty Frame. Following these Teaching Notes is an assignment which one can use to complement the exercise. Especially in schools where resources are constrained, this permits sharing the gallery in a way that is cost-efficient. Suggested text for the assignment appears as Model Assignment 1 in the Teaching Notes appendix.

Creative Dialogue: Invite students to choose two writings from the anthology and imagine what the authors of those two works might say to each other. Suggested text for such an assignment appears in Model Assignment 2 in the Teaching Notes appendix.

A Framework for Collecting and Sharing Voices on Important Contemporary Issues: We have chronicled our creation journey in the article: Schoen, M., Reardon, K. and Longo, J. "Lift Every Voice: An

Anthology of Contemporary Student Writings on Race" The WAC Journal, Vol 28: 7-33 (2017). We encourage our readers to think about using this process to collect voices on issues important to their institutions and communities.

IN LIVING COLOR: AN ANTHOLOGY

TEACHING NOTES APPENDIX
Model Assignment 1

Course: MBA Frameworks for Socially Responsible Decision-Making

Assignment: Reflective Exercise on the Poetry Gallery-Go Wide and Deep

This is a required assignment and should be posted online before our next class. It counts as part of your class participation for the Go Wide and Deep experience.

Before leaving class, please think about and make some notes in response to the following questions for use in completing the associated assignment.

1. What did you/did you not talk about that surprised you?

2. Did you *feel* any different after the exercise than before?

3. Was there something you saw in or heard from in others that you hadn't seen/heard before?

4. Did the experience shed light on any of the major themes (e.g., ethics, law, conflicts, risk, liability leadership, stress, communication, diversity, status, duty, social responsibility) of our course?

5. Did the experience change any of your opinions or feelings?

In a two-page paper, follow Kolb's Experiential Learning Cycle described below (See Osland et al., 2004) to reflect on and describe your progressive participation in tonight's gallery experience as well as to trace some aspect of your own learning.

Concrete Experience: Describe your experience with the gallery, in your small group, and with the full class.

Reflexive Observation: Reflect on the entirety of the experience from the different perspectives.

Abstract Conceptualization: Theorize or conceptualize the experience in the coming week as you read Chapter One which introduces the course material.

Active Experimentation: This is your opportunity to reflect on the experience and what you might do differently in a similar situation in the future. Describe and reflect on the experience, but also explain and make sense of it.

REFERENCES

Osland, J., Rubin, I., Kolb, D., & Turner, M. (2004). *Organizational behavior: An experiential approach.* New York, NY: Prentice Hall.

Exercise prepared by Karen A. Reardon, PhD, JD based on Van Buskirk, W. and London, M. *(2012).* Poetry as deep intelligence: A qualitative approach for the organizational behavior classroom. *Journal of Management Education, 36,* 636-668.

TEACHING NOTES APPENDIX
Model Assignment 2

Course: The Human Person- An Introductory Philosophy Class
Assignment: Reflective Essay/Dialogue

Assignment: For this assignment, you will reflect on an issue or question raised by **two** of the texts we have studied by bringing two of the figures we have studied so far into dialogue with each other as detailed below in 1-2 pages typed, single-spaced, in 12-pt font (pref. Times New Roman).

Details: Craft an original dialogue between two of the figures we have studied so far this semester (Socrates, Thomas Aquinas, Martin Luther King, Jr., and Malcolm X). Your dialogue should focus on a central question or topic relevant to *both* figures' work or concerns, and should illuminate important points of correspondence and/or contrast between their positions. While you should refer to the assigned texts to capture the style and philosophical positions of the figures, the substance of the exchange between them should be original (i.e., do not use direct quotes). However, please include page and/or line references from the texts we have studied following any substantive claims they make in the dialogue. Your dialogue may follow the format Plato gives us (in Socrates' exchange with Meletus in the *Apology*, for example, or in his exchange with Crito in the *Crito*), or the format Thomas employs (i.e., with an opening question, objections, answer and replies), or it may take a more contemporary format (e.g., Twitter war).

Formatting and content guidelines:

For the dialogue:

> ➢ Include your full name in the top, left-hand corner of the first page, along with the course number and section and the name of the assignment, Dialogue. Example: Katy Did

PHL 151.21

Dialogue

➢ **This is a short writing assignment, so it is critical that you focus your work on one or two key points that you develop in your writing.** I strongly suggest that you decide on and work through these points in advance of writing, and then organize your assignment around those points.

➢ Your essay or dialogue should represent your own work. Avoid consulting internet sources. Violations of the Academic Integrity Policy will be reported, and will result in an F for the assignment.

➢ Your essay or dialogue should draw on specific passages that support your thesis or the claims the figures make. Please include parenthetical citations so that I know where to find the passage you are referring to. Place the parenthetical citation at the end of the sentence, and include in it the page number.

Example: Socrates describes himself as a "gadfly" (33).

Since this is a short writing assignment, avoid quoting long passages.

Tips for writing dialogue:

➢ Make sure you understand each figures' position on the topic you are focusing on before you begin writing. Everything these figures say to each other should be consistent with their respective positions.

➢ With reference to the style of the texts we have studied, try to capture the "voice" of each figure in their exchange.

➢ Give your dialogue a title that specifies the topic it is focused on.

Adapted from an assignment developed by Whitely Howell, PhD for the La Salle University undergraduate introductory philosophy course PHL 151. This is the assignment which produced the Unit 7 piece entitled "Cycle of Violence" in which student author Daniel Gomez shares a conversation between Socrates and Malcolm X.

Cover Image: Moe Brooker (b. 1940), *Might Could*, 2000. Oil and Pastel on Paper, 30" x 30". Purchased with funds provided by Michael Duffy, Dr. Helen North, Dr. Dennis O'Brien, and the Morrow-Farrell Family (in memory of Theodore Eggleston Morrow), Collection of La Salle University Art Museum, 05-D-414. Artwork © Moe Brooker.

About the Artist and his Artwork:

Philadelphia artist Moe Brooker approaches art-making as an inventive process of developing and working through ideas. His colorful abstractions express a joyous, spiritual energy and a spontaneity inspired by the harmonies of jazz music. Brooker writes in his artist's statement,

> My work is about the joy of the human spirit. Joy is not happiness but a deep abiding knowledge; a "knowing" that is way down deep inside each person. My paintings are about rhythmic patterns and layered, colorful surfaces that reflect my belief in the human spirit.
>
> Issues that guide and impact me are of a spiritual nature. Jazz is spiritual, poetry is spiritual and for me, so is painting. My joy is an embrace of life, of God, the universe and humanity. Formally, I attempt to create visual harmonies and jazz is often a metaphor. My work is really a celebration of life. Each person lives life according to his or her beliefs. I believe in a higher being and choose to worship that being through my work. Working in my studio is worship. I want my work to communicate; I don't ask you to like the work, I dare you to engage it.

To look, to touch, to feel and then to know is my quest, which I believe is the quest of humanity. Isn't this why we love and hurt and feel so deeply? For within me, in all of us, is the potential of every human being. If I speak to those things in me, I can speak to others.

I think of my work as maps that take you on a journey through an imagined universe filled with moments of joy, sadness, pleasure and delight. My works are an attempt to share my journey and perhaps stir the sense of the human journey that we all take.

Among other honors, Brooker received the 2010 Governor's Hazlett Memorial Award for Artist of the Year by the Pennsylvania Council on the Arts. He studied at the Pennsylvania Academy of the Fine Arts and Temple University's Tyler School of Arts. He is currently a professor emeritus at Moore College of Art in Philadelphia. *Might Could* was recently featured in the exhibition, *Approaching Abstraction: African American Art from the Permanent Collection,* at La Salle University Art Museum, March 15–June 15, 2017.

About La Salle University Art Museum:

La Salle University Art Museum (LSUAM) is a place of community engagement, educational inquiry, and interdisciplinary exploration -- offering visitors of all ages and from all walks of life, opportunities to learn about original artworks, their historical contexts, and their continuing relevance. LSUAM began in 1965 as an educational resource for students, as well as for the communities in the surrounding area. The core collection includes a comprehensive selection of European and American art from the Renaissance to the present, as well as additional special collections of non-Western and ancient art. The collection is housed in a series of period rooms in the lower level of Olney Hall on the University's main campus. LSUAM presents high-quality exhibitions, lectures and educational programs for the La Salle community as well as broader public audiences, including underserved preK-12 school groups and special needs groups. These activities support the University's Catholic Lasallian mission of experiential education, social justice, and service to the community.

POSTSCRIPT

"If you can't fly then run, if you can't run then walk, if you can't walk then crawl, but whatever you do you have to keep moving forward."

The exact origin of this phrase is not known, though it is reported that it appeared in the book of the prophet Isaiah for the first time, but later Dr. Martin Luther King used it in his famous speech at a Spelman college rally in Sisters Chapel. He says;

> Keep moving, for it may well be that the greatest song has not yet been sung, the greatest book has not been written, the highest mountain has not been climbed. This is your challenge! Reach out and grab it… but there is something we can learn from the broken grammar of that mother, that we must keep moving. If you can't fly, run; if you can't run, walk; if you can't walk, crawl; but by all means keep moving.

… The words fly, run, walk, and crawl all have a sense of purpose, of perseverance, a call to not settle when option "A" doesn't work but to try options B and C and D, if necessary. It is that sense of purpose that we wish to rekindle in all of us, but we also want to focus that purpose. Dr. King helps us do that with another quote:

> Make a career of humanity. Commit yourself to the noble struggle for equal rights. You will make a greater person of yourself, a greater nation of your country, and a finer world to live in.

This sense of purpose, this perseverance is about the common good, *the noble struggle for equal rights* for all individuals… we must learn to not just talk but to crawl, to walk, to run and to fly when it comes *to* making *a finer world to live in*….

Excerpted from the writing by Brother Robert Kinzler, FSC
for the La Salle University King's Dream Committee 2017

THE CHALLENGE

How will each of us leave this world?
How will each of us act to make our world better,
more just,
more equal
simply because we have passed through?

Made in United States
North Haven, CT
28 May 2024